and
THE TEN COMMANDMENTS

A WARNING FOR THESE TIMES

E. Mary Christie

Preserving
Christian
Publications
(315) 942-6617

Preserving Christian Publications
P.O. Box 221
Boonville, New York 13309
United States
Tel: 1-315-942-6617
Email: info@pcpbooks.com
https://www.pcpbooks.net

ISBN 978-1-7343775-9-0

Sculpture by the Italian High Renaissance artist,
Michelangelo Buonarroti (c. 1513–1515),
housed in the Church of San Pietro in Vincoli in Rome,
depicting Moses with horns on his head to remind us
of the sacred Altar of Incense that God told Moses to have built,
bearing a horn at each corner, calling to mind
that God is the horn of our Salvation.[1]

---

[1] Psalm 17:13.

TABLE OF CONTENTS

PREFACE

In these times of the twenty-first century wherein attempts are being made to vilify God's Commandments to suit the dictates of modern man, it begs the question: why are we altering the sacred precepts of God's holy instruction provided as a cure to bring sinful man back into full communion with Him? Are we not fearful of invoking God's anger over such defiance, like what happened to the inhabitants of Sodom and Gomorrha[1] when they broke God's law by committing the sin of sodomy? Can we not see the insidious wiles of Satan, dragging souls into damnation by corrupting man's thinking to accept as normality[2] that which destroyed these two ancient cities?

We have only to review the first book of the Old Testament where Adam and Eve failed God's test of obedience (tempted as they were by Satan) to draw a clear parallel with this same evil force dominating our world today.

Yet even without this foresight, surely we should be on our guard as we see the destruction of God's holy Commandments and many of the traditional sacred precepts, such wickedness born of bowing to the kingship of man as opposed to the Kingship of Christ. If we don't fight against these evils, it further begs the question: what will happen if we continue to fall prey to the insidious wiles of the devil, drawing souls away from obeying the Word of God?

---

[1] Jude 1:7.

[2] Disguised under the title of 'same sex unions'.

As we progress now to the story of Moses (chosen by God to rescue the enslaved Israelites in Egypt) we are woefully provided with the answer.

Yet even so, it is a story that will hopefully encourage all souls to fight to defend the traditional Faith that Jesus Christ instituted upon the earth—enabling the prophecy of Ezechiel[3] to be fulfilled. A prophecy interpreted by St. Bonaventure wherein our world will then see a complete restoration of the social Kingship of Christ—thereby rescuing all misled souls and setting them upon the path of holiness toward the Promised Land in the Kingdom of Heaven.

---

[3] Ezechiel, Chapters 40-43.

Altar of Incense (Exodus 37:25)

Exodus 2:11

Chapter 1
GOD'S CALLING
Gratitude

As we commence our tour of the Old Testament in search of Moses, chosen by God to free the Israelites from their life of slavery in Egypt and lead them to the Promised Land, we first learn that Moses came from a long line of Israelites, his forefathers going back as far as Abraham (the ancient patriarch with whom God made a covenant that he would be a father of many nations[1]).

In order to ascertain how and in what way the Israelites became slaves in Egypt, we learn from the book of Genesis[2] that one of Abraham's descendants was an Israelite named Joseph, who was the youngest of all of his half-brothers. As their father Jacob appeared to favor Joseph, a number of these brethren were envious of their favored brother. And as happens when the sin of envy snakes its way into the soul, these same brethren cast Joseph (at the time sixteen years old) into a deep pit[3] that he may die. However, in spotting a caravan of foreign merchants (who happened to be passing by with their camels, carrying spices, balm and myrrh to Egypt) they hastily drew him out of the pit and sold him to the Ismaelites.

Once taken to that foreign land, Joseph was sold as a servant to one of Pharaoh's Egyptian officers,[4] and in due time found favor with Pharaoh after he interpreted the king's

---

[1] Genesis 17:2-5.

[2] Genesis 37:3-4.

[3] Genesis 37:18-28.

[4] Genesis 37:36 (referred to as Pharao in the Douay-Rheims, not as spelled above).

1

dreams.[5] He was then granted a high place in Pharaoh's kingdom and ended up leading a happy and successful life.

Over time, the Israelites grew to a very large number, increasing from generation to generation (as promised by God would happen to the seed of Abraham). Indeed, on opening the book of Exodus, from its very first chapter we learn that Egypt became home to an ever-increasing population of Israelites.

Returning to our search for Moses, these same passages[6] lead us into a time when a jealous king took over the land, one who the evil serpent had smitten with a desire for wealth and power. On perceiving the vast number of Israelites, the king feared that they may become more powerful than the Egyptians, and would seek to take over his kingdom. He had also heard of their God, whom the Israelites believed was more powerful than the pagan god that he worshipped. He sat on his throne and pondered what he should do.

It didn't take long before Satan provided him with a plan. He would reduce the number of the Israelites by making slaves of their menfolk and force them to build two cities containing vast storehouses to contain his treasures. He promptly appointed taskmasters and overseers and ordered them to round up the Israelites and get them to work right away. The Israelites were then treated most cruelly, watched over by Pharaoh's slave-drivers who worked them from morning to night, leaving them little time to eat and rest, and would beat them mercilessly at little or no provocation. Yet in spite of their

---

[5] Genesis 41:39-41.

[6] Exodus 1:8-14.

great suffering at the hands of their Egyptian oppressors, the Israelite numbers continued to grow.

So the conniving serpent whispered into the sinful soul of Pharaoh, suggesting a further evil plan—in response to which the king next ordered that all of the newly born Israelite male babies were to be drowned at birth[7] (his new plan not dissimilar to that which is in our sinful world today, promoting the abortion of the unborn in a bid to reduce the world's population).

Returning to the wicked king's plan of attack on the Israelites, we note that God in His infinite mercy then implemented His own plan (one that not only would free the Israelites from their life of bondage, but in due time called for the protection of all innocent life[8]). As we follow God's divine plan, we first learn[9] that one of the Israelites, a courageous mother named Jochabed,[10] having given birth to a baby boy, was determined to hide him from the Egyptians. However, after three months, as her child's cries grew stronger, Jochabed feared that he would soon be discovered. So, clearly guided by Providence, she thought of a way to save her baby.

Having learned that the childless daughter of Pharaoh would go down to the River Nile to wash in its waters each day, Jochabed placed her baby (while he slept) in a wicker basket lined with pitch and padded with straw, and taking her daughter with her, headed over to the river. Praying that God would save her child, she set the basinet upon the waters at a

---

[7] Exodus 1:22.

[8] Being one of the sacred precepts of God's Ten Commandments.

[9] Exodus 2:1-10.

[10] Jochabid, married to Amram (Exodus 6:18-20).

hidden spot up the river, a short distance from where the princess and her maids would come to bathe. She then gently pushed the basket so that it floated down the river towards the spot, and instructed her daughter to follow along the river-bank so that she could report back to her mother.

As the basket drifted down the Nile, it got caught in the bulrushes lining the riverbank. While the young girl wondered what she should do, she suddenly heard laughter and happy chatter as the daughter of Pharaoh and her two maids arrived on the scene. At the same time, her baby brother awoke and started crying, which promptly drew attention to the basket.

At the command of the princess, her maids hastily retrieved it—and lifting the lid, they beheld the beautiful baby within. The princess straight away fell in love with the child, and wanted to keep him as her own. Lifting the baby into her arms, she decided to name him 'Moses'—perhaps from the Egyptian word *mes* meaning 'son'. As the princess was unable to comfort the baby's hungry wailing, the young girl ran up and said that she knew someone who could nurse the baby—to which Pharaoh's daughter told her to call the nurse right away. Even if the princess suspected it would be the child's own mother, she was determined to keep the baby.

And so Moses grew up in Pharaoh's royal household, with his own mother employed as his nurse during his infancy. He never knew that he was an Israelite until, at forty years of age, it was secretly revealed to him. By then, already a young man with his own horse and chariot, Moses straight away sought out his Israelite kinsmen who were employed on

God's Calling
Gratitude

Pharaoh's construction site.[11] On arrival, Moses promptly witnessed the merciless cruelty being inflicted on the teams of slaves being forced to haul huge blocks of brick towards the site where other slaves were working on creating the cities.

At one point, as the teams moved on, Moses spotted the fallen figure of an Israelite being beaten by one of the overseers, even as the man's broken body lay prostrate on the ground. His fiery spirit sparked by such injustice, Moses impetuously drew forth his spear and hurled it at the Egyptian—instantly killing him. Afraid of the repercussions of his action (and believing that no one had seen him) Moses quickly hid the Egyptian's body by burying it in the sand.

The following day he again took his chariot and went over to the building site, where he found two Israelites arguing with each other. As Moses stepped forward in an attempt to stop their contentious exchange, one of them made reference to Moses' act of killing the Egyptian overseer the previous day. Afraid that Pharaoh would hear of the incident, and knowing that he would be angry and have him killed, Moses promptly fled for his life.

He ended up in the Sinai Peninsula, land of the Madianites[12]—and in that foreign place, sat pondering his fate by a well, when along came seven young maidens bringing their father's flock for water.[13] As Moses watched, other shepherds came and sought to drive them away—at which

---

[11] Exodus 2:11-15.

[12] Madianites, descendants of Madian, son of Abraham and Cetura; his siblings were Zamran, Jecsan, Madan, Jesboc, and a sister named Sue; their half-brother was Isaac born to Abraham's first wife Sara (Genesis 25:1-2; 1 Paralipomenon 1:32).

[13] Exodus 2:16-20.

point Moses jumped up, his fiery spirit once again sparked by the injustice, and promptly defended the maidens, so that their sheep were quickly watered that day.

When the maidens told their father Jethro (who was a priest of Madian) what had happened, he asked why they had left the kind stranger behind, saying that he wanted to make his acquaintance—and he sent them back to find the young man. Moses then happily returned with the maidens, whereupon Jethro warmly welcomed him into his household, treating him as one of his own. Furthermore, he gave Moses a herd of goats and sheep to tender.

So Moses now had a new life as a shepherd with the nomadic tribe of the Madianites—from whom he would have learned all about God, for unlike the Egyptians (who worshipped false gods) Jethro's family of Israelites had a history of devotion to Almighty God. In due time,[14] Moses married one of Jethro's daughters, Sephora. Their first son, Moses named Gersam (meaning 'stranger in this foreign land') and their second son, Moses named Eliezer (meaning 'help of God') declaring:

"For the God of my father, my helper, hath delivered me out of the hand of Pharao[h]."

Hence, we see Moses not only as a man of compassion for those being treated unjustly, but one who had already acquired the virtue of a humble *gratitude* to Almighty God—not only for saving him from the sword of Pharaoh, but also for removing him from the pagan lifestyle of riches and wealth in favor of a simple life surrounded by the riches of God's creation and

---

[14] Exodus 2:21-23.

goodness (as seen in Moses' humble acceptance of his new life as a lowly shepherd).

Exodus 3:2

Chapter 2
THE BURNING BUSH
Submission to God's Holy Will

After some many years, the wicked king of Egypt passed on from this life, although the Israelites remained in captivity under a new and equally cruel Pharaoh who, like the previous one was similarly driven by the spirit of Satan, inflicting his soul with a desire for wealth and power. So the Israelites cried out to God to help them[1]—but of course God already had a plan in place, not only to free His people from slavery, but one that would help to free mankind from their bondage in sin.

Unaware of God's plan for the world, Moses as usual was tending his flock when his steps led him into the inner parts of the desert and up Mount Sinai[2] (also known as Mount Horeb and which later became known as God's 'Holy Mountain').

Continuing with the story,[3] while his flock grazed on the mountain slopes, Moses happened to spot something strange in the near distance that promptly caught his attention. What he saw was a burning bush which appeared to be on fire—yet its leaves remained intact in spite of the flames engulfing it. Leaving his flock, Moses climbed the rocky surface to get a closer look at this strange phenomenon. As he approached, the bright flame caused him to shield his eyes—when suddenly from within, he heard an echoing voice calling out to him:

"Moses, Moses!"

---

[1] Exodus 2:23.

[2] Exodus 3:1.

[3] Exodus 3:2-22.

The Burning Bush
Submission to God's Holy Will

Scarcely believing the evidence of his own ears, we can imagine an awe-struck Moses now stammering:

"Here I am!"

The mysterious voice continued, cautioning Moses to come no further:

"Put off the shoes from thy feet: for the place whereon thou standest is holy ground."

Throwing off his sandals, Moses promptly fell to his knees as the echoing voice continued:

"I am the God of thy father, the God of Abraham, the God of Isaac, and the God of Jacob… I have seen the affliction of my people in Egypt, and I have heard their cry… and knowing their sorrow, I am come down to deliver them out of the hands of the Egyptians, and to bring them out of that land into a good and spacious land, into a land that floweth with milk and honey."

By this time, Moses had his face to the earth, for he dared not look into the flame of God's fire. The voice of Almighty God then provided Moses with a clear instruction:

"I will send thee to Pharao[h], that thou mayst bring forth my people, the children of Israel out of Egypt."

Much troubled at the daunting prospect of such a mission, his voice trembling, Moses dared to ask:

"Who am I that I should go to Pharao[h], and should bring forth the children of Israel out of Egypt?"

But God's voice comforted him:

"I will be with thee: and this thou shalt have for a sign, that I have sent thee: When thou shalt have brought my people out of Egypt, thou shalt offer a sacrifice to God upon this mountain."

The Burning Bush
Submission to God's Holy Will

Still stammering, Moses responded:

"Lo, I shall go to the children of Israel, and say to them: The God of your fathers hath sent me to you; if they should say to me: what is His name, what shall I say to them?"

In the words all too familiar to biblical scholars, God said to Moses:

"I AM WHO AM. Thus shalt thou say to the children of Israel: The Lord God of your fathers, the God of Abraham, the God of Isaac, and the God of Jacob, hath sent me to you."

And God further assured Moses that He would be with him when he approached Pharaoh to let His people go free, and even though the stubborn-minded Pharaoh would not at first agree, God would stretch forth His Hand and strike Egypt in such a way that the king would eventually let the Israelites go.

However, as we follow the story[4] we see that Moses was clearly troubled, for he now appealed to God:

"They will not believe me, nor hear my voice, but they will say: The Lord hath not appeared to thee."

The echoing voice of the Almighty then drew attention to the shepherd's staff that Moses was holding in his hand, saying to him:

"Cast it down upon the ground."

And having cast the rod down, it promptly turned into a writhing snake, causing Moses to jump back in horror. Even so, the voice of Almighty God continued:

"Put out thy hand and take it by the tail."

---

[4] Exodus 4:1-17.

11

The Burning Bush
Submission to God's Holy Will

Hesitating but for a moment, Moses put forth his hand as God instructed—whereupon the snake turned back into the rod!

This would be a miracle to help Moses convince Pharaoh that the God of the Israelites was truly present and that the king was to listen and obey Him. And to show His chosen servant that He would always be his guiding Hand, God wrought a further miracle for Moses by making him put his own hand into his coat against his chest—whereupon on withdrawing it, it turned snowy white. As Moses stared at his hand, God told him to put it back into his coat and withdraw again—whereupon it returned to its normal color.

Yet even so, Moses was understandably still troubled, believing that after all these years as a lowly shepherd, he had not the gift of eloquence and knew not how he would be able to converse with Pharaoh in a way that he would listen to him.

Now God knew that back in Egypt, Moses had an older brother named Aaron[5]—a man who was head of the Israelite priesthood and was well versed in the art of communication. So God told Moses that He would appoint Aaron to assist him in addressing Pharaoh, and that He would bring Aaron to meet Moses as he journeyed back to Egypt. Bowing his head in all humility, Moses then meekly accepted God's holy Will.

Returning to his flock, Moses hastily shepherded them back to camp, to share with his trustworthy father-in-law all that he had just heard and witnessed.[6] The priest of Madian

---

[5] Aaron—first high priest of Israel; brother of Moses and his sister Mary [Miriam], and eldest son of Amram and Jochabed (Exodus 6:20).

[6] Exodus 4:18-20.

listened carefully to all that Moses told him. As a priestly man of God, Jethro had no doubt that it was the Lord God of Israel who had spoken to Moses—and he encouraged him to take his family and return to Egypt, saying:

"Go in peace."

So Moses (now an elderly man of eighty), armed with his rod, set forth on his journey, taking with him his wife Sephora and their two grown sons, together with an ass and their belongings—thus to embark on the mission that the Lord God had assigned to him.

And just as God had promised,[7] on the way to Egypt, Aaron (believed to have been in his eighty-third year) came forth into the desert at God's command, and met up with Moses. We can imagine their joyous greeting, for the brothers had never known each other (given that Moses had been brought up in the king's household as the adopted son of Pharaoh's daughter during his time in Egypt).

Deeply humbled by God's infinite goodness in bringing them together, the brothers set forth to accomplish what God was calling them to do.

Thus we see Moses' lowly *submission to God's holy Will*—in spite of the enormity of what God wanted him and Aaron to do.

---

[7] Exodus 4:27-28.

Exodus 7:10

Chapter 3
TEN PLAGUES
Trust

We next learn that on their arrival back in the land of Egypt,[1] Moses had Aaron summon together the ancients among the Israelites and reveal to them the words that Almighty God had spoken to him through the flame of a burning bush—and each of them believed. Giving praise and thanksgiving, they expressed their firm belief that God would be working to set them free.

Moses and Aaron then went to speak to the king,[2] telling him that their God—the God of the Israelites—had commanded that he let His people go that they may journey three days into the wilderness to make sacrifices to their Lord God. But Pharaoh's response was one of scorn:

"Who is the Lord, that I should hear his voice, and let Israel go? I know not the Lord, neither will I let Israel go."

And he promptly dismissed Moses and Aaron from his presence.

The snake of contempt having crept into Pharaoh's arrogant soul (over what he deemed as Moses and Aaron's outrageous audacity) he then issued a new order,[3] one that forced the Israelites to gather their own straw required to make the building bricks for the construction site, while at the same time they were to produce them within the same time-frame as before. As the lives of the Israelites were now made even more difficult, they complained to Moses and Aaron, whereupon

---

[1] Exodus 4:29-31.

[2] Exodus 5:1-4.

[3] Exodus 5:5-18.

Ten Plagues
Trust

Moses appealed to the Lord God and was promptly told to not give up[4]—that by the Hand of Almighty God, the wicked Pharaoh would release the Israelites in due time. And God instructed His faithful servant to return to the king with Aaron, this time with a warning[5] that if Pharaoh failed to release the Israelites, their Lord God would punish him.

At this, Pharaoh insisted that they give him a sign to prove that their God was more powerful than his magicians. So Moses had Aaron throw down his staff, which (as Moses had witnessed on Mount Sinai) promptly turned into a writhing snake. But as Pharaoh's magicians (who were able to work a certain measure of magic) similarly turned their staffs into snakes, this had little effect on the stubborn king. As the snakes wriggled and writhed all over the floor, he sneeringly looked down his nose at Moses and Aaron—whereupon God promptly made the serpent, produced by the rod of Moses, devour each and every one of the magicians' snakes, and before Pharaoh's wide-eyed audience, then turned it back into the rod of Moses. Angry over what he perceived as an assault against his magicians, the enraged king promptly dismissed God's servants.

Not to be outdone, the very next day, in response to God's further instruction,[6] Moses and Aaron waited on the bank of the River Nile, and when Pharaoh and his servants appeared, they told the king that if he was still not prepared to release the Israelites, their Lord God would turn the waters of the river into blood—that Pharaoh may understand that God the

---

[4] Exodus 6:1-8.

[5] Exodus 7:10-13.

[6] Exodus 7:15-25.

Almighty was calling on him to obey. Alas, in the king's belief that his magicians could accomplish the same feat, their words were promptly greeted by another mocking sneer. So Moses had Aaron touch the waters with the tip of his rod—whereupon, as the Lord had warned, the waters straight away turned to BLOOD; this being the *First Plague*.

Yet the obstinate Pharaoh was still not impressed, believing that his magicians would be able to restore the waters. Turning on his heel, he walked away. For seven days, however, the bloodied waters remained, the magicians unable to do as the king thought they could. Indeed, all the waters in both lakes and ponds, and even that which was contained in stone pots and jars became as blood. All of the fish died and everywhere people had to dig down into the earth to find fresh water that they could drink. After seven days (having granted Pharaoh sufficient time to understand the power of Almighty God) the Lord then restored all of the waters throughout Egypt.

In the hope that the king was now convinced (and as further directed by God) Moses and Aaron returned to Pharaoh,[7] once again requesting that he release the Israelites. But the king remained stubborn in his refusal. Not even the threat that God would send down a plague of frogs if he continued to refuse, had any effect on the unbending Pharaoh. So the following morning, as predicted, the king awoke to find FROGS all over his bed. Indeed the frogs were everywhere, throughout his palace and in all of the Egyptians' homes; this *Second Plague* causing much annoyance and misery throughout the land—for while Pharaoh's magicians were able to produce

---

[7] Exodus 8:1-15.

frogs, they were not able to remove these that God had brought down upon the Egyptians as a result of the king's disobedience.

Irritated by the sight of the frogs, Pharaoh called upon Moses and Aaron and told them to have their God remove the blight of this annoying plague—and in return, he would release the Israelites. In light of the king's seeming change of heart, Moses promised that God would remove the frogs at a certain hour the following day—to prove to Pharaoh that the plague had been removed by the Hand of Almighty God. And sure enough, at the appointed time, all of the frogs in every place and corner, promptly dropped down dead. Even so, his pagan heart still beholden to Satan, Pharaoh remained unbending. He refused to be impressed (or even grateful)—and nor would he release the Israelites.

That we may learn from such disobedience, God called upon Moses[8] to have Aaron stretch forth his rod to touch the dirt—which immediately blew forth a cloud of GNATS; this being the *Third Plague*. The swarming gnats, just like the frogs, irritated Pharaoh to the core for as insects drawn to carbon dioxide exhaled by humans, the gnats stung his face and the faces of all of the Egyptians; and similarly caused much grief to their cattle and other beasts. The king's magicians of course were unable to remove that which God had sent down upon the earth; in fact, the magicians told Pharaoh that they believed the plague had been brought on by the God of the Israelites—which only served to make the rebellious king even more angry, and hardened his heart all the more.

---

[8] Exodus 8:16-19.

Ten Plagues
Trust

We next learn[9] that God called upon Moses to arise early and go again to the bank of the Nile, where He would send Pharaoh and his servants. When the king arrived, Moses approached him, reiterating that the Almighty was still calling on him to let the Israelites go—and if he continued to refuse, God would send down a plague of flies. As these words were once again greeted with yet another obstinate refusal, come the morning a swarm of FLIES came upon the land—this *Fourth Plague* filling the king's palace and every Egyptian home with its grievous infestation. Not however, the homes of the Israelites and the land within which they dwelt (popularly known as Goshen[10])—God's way of putting a division between His people and the godless Egyptians, that the stubborn Pharaoh may recognize that the God of the Israelites was in control.

Greatly aggravated by this further plague, the king called on Moses and Aaron and told them that he would release the Israelites—but first, before leaving, they were to pray to their Lord God to remove this pestilence. Alas, in line with Pharaoh's typically deceitful *modus operandi*, it comes as no surprise that in spite of God removing this plague,[11] Pharaoh reneged on his promise.

As the king remained unrepentant, the Almighty then sent down a *Fifth Plague*—being that of a BLIGHT on the livestock; a most grievous murrain that killed many of the cattle, horses, asses, camels and sheep,[12] although once again

---

[9] Exodus 8:20-31.

[10] Referred to as Gessen in the Douay-Rheims.

[11] Exodus 8:32.

[12] Exodus 9:1-7.

not those that belonged to God's people, whose animals stayed healthy and strong. Nevertheless, in spite of this terrible plague, Pharaoh would not surrender. (Oh the hard-heartedness of this stubborn king!)

So God commanded Moses and Aaron[13] to take handfuls of ash from out of the chimney—and in the presence of Pharaoh, Moses was to sprinkle them into the air. The effect of this brought down the *Sixth Plague,* being that of BOILS on the people and beasts, including the magicians whose magic of course was not able to heal their affliction. Even so, as the events unfold, all too clearly we see the obstinacy of Pharaoh, his heart continuing to be enslaved by the evil one.

Compelled to take things a stage further, God next called upon Moses and Aaron to appear before Pharaoh[14] to warn of a terrible storm that would destroy all of the crops—in fact both man and creature would be killed in the onslaught of its destruction. (At this warning, one may be tempted to believe that Pharaoh would surely let God's people go to thereby avoid such devastation.) But the rebellious king still refused to take heed—not even when Moses warned him to advise his people to take necessary precautions for themselves and their beasts as the storm would hit Egypt the following day.

In light of Pharaoh's continuing defiance, the next morning at God's command, Moses stretched forth his rod towards Heaven, whereupon the skies promptly clouded over and there appeared streaks of fiery lightning, accompanied by crashing thunder. And God rained down HAIL throughout the

---

[13] Exodus 9:8-12.

[14] Exodus 9:13-35.

land of Egypt, this *Seventh Plague* like nothing they had ever seen before. It broke trees and destroyed plants and crops, along with people and beasts that had failed to take cover. Only the land of Goshen, home of the Israelites, escaped the storm.

In the face of this total devastation, we next see the sleezy tactics of Satan calling on the king to summon Moses and Aaron—whereupon Pharaoh told them:

"I have sinned this time also; the Lord is just: I and my people are wicked. Pray ye to the Lord, that the thunderings of God and the hail may cease: that I may let you go, and that you may stay here no longer."

On hearing this seemingly humble confession, Moses went forth and beseeched God to end the storm. Yet the storm having ended, we see Pharaoh's heart still ensnared by Satan (the father of all lies) for he once again reneged on his promise. So Moses and Aaron returned to Pharaoh,[15] this time warning him that if he refused to release the Israelites, God would inflict on the Egyptians a plague of locusts. And in clear detail, they warned Pharaoh that these locusts would consume all that had remained after the hailstorm—their magnitude like as none other known, not in the time of their fathers nor grandfathers and long before them.

As soon as Moses and Aaron left the king, his servants having overheard the warning, turned to Pharaoh beseeching him to let the Israelites go for already their land had suffered a massive destruction. Pharaoh then summoned Moses and Aaron back into his presence, and in the sight of his servants asked how many Israelites would be needed to make the

---

[15] Exodus 10:3-12.

required sacrifices to their Lord God—to which Moses responded:

"We will go with our young and old, with our sons and daughters, with our sheep and herds: for it is the solemnity of the Lord our God."

At this, the king angrily snorted:

"It shall not be so! But go ye men only, and sacrifice to the Lord."

And he dismissed them.

Immediately after they left, God told Moses to stretch forth his rod over the land—whereupon a burning wind sprang up which blew for the rest of that day and into the night. Come morning, the *Eighth Plague,* being a vast number of LOCUSTS appeared,[16] swarming across the fields and the land. We can imagine the king awakening to the sound of locusts thumping all over his rooftop—for they filled the air and were everywhere. Being locusts, they devoured all the crops in the fields and everything green and edible that had survived the hailstorm. The Egyptians no doubt would have complained out loud—for Pharaoh then hastily summoned Moses and Aaron, this time professing a seemingly more contrite confession:

"I have sinned against the Lord your God, and against you. But now forgive me my sin this time also, and pray to the Lord your God, that He take away from me this death."

Going forth from Pharaoh's presence, Moses prayed that God would take away this plague—in response to which a strong wind blew across the land, taking with it each and every

---

[16] Exodus 10:13-20.

locust so that they were no more. Yet again Satan's faithful servant refused to obey God's commandment—such was the further dishonest confession that Pharaoh had made to Moses and Aaron.

And as what happens to the soul when blackened after a dishonest confession, the Lord God brought down an intense DARKNESS over the land, which *Ninth Plague* covered Egypt for three whole days[17]—an intensity of darkness wherein none could move from the place where they were (except the Israelites whose area remained in the light). Angry that he and his household were unable to venture forth, Pharaoh called Moses and Aaron to appear before him, this time saying:

"Go sacrifice to the Lord; let your sheep only, and herds remain; let your children go with you."

However, Moses told Pharaoh most firmly that the sheep and herds were to go with them for these would be needed as food, and as burnt offerings to the Lord their God; all that belonged to the Israelites were to go with them. At this, Pharaoh was enraged. He told Moses and Aaron that he wished never to see them again. No longer were they to appear before him, else he would order their death—to which Moses responded:

"So shall it be as thou hast spoken, I will not see thy face anymore."

In light of all of the above, God told Moses that one last plague He would bring down upon Pharaoh and his people.[18] On a designated midnight, He would pass over the land of

---

[17] Exodus 10:21-29.

[18] Exodus 11:1-10.

Egypt and would kill every firstborn Egyptian, both man and beast—to include Pharaoh's own son. And God assured His faithful servant that after this *Tenth Plague* of DEATH to the Egyptians' first-born, Pharaoh would release the Israelites, and He provided Moses with careful instructions to prepare the people for their exodus from Egypt.[19]

On the tenth day of that month, every family was to take to themselves a lamb—one without blemish, a male, one year old—which they were to keep until the fourteenth day of that same month, at which time they were to sacrifice it in the evening. Taking the blood of the sacrificed lamb, they were to sprinkle it on all sides of their outer door-frames that God may know that they had obeyed and would pass over their homes, keeping their firstborn safe—this night to be remembered as the Phase (the Passage) of the Lord's passing.

True to God's Word, after His people had done as the Lord had commanded (and after they had eaten the flesh of the sacrificed lamb in accordance with His further specific instructions) that very same midnight God passed over Egypt taking the life of every firstborn Egyptian—including Pharaoh's own son.

The following morning—devastated, distraught, and apparently chastened—Pharaoh now ordered the Israelites be gone from his land! And to take their livestock and possessions with them—for at last, it would seem, he feared their Lord God. The Egyptian people were similarly fearful, offering the Israelites vessels of silver and gold as they bid them depart with all speed lest they should all die.

---

[19] Exodus 12:1-37.

Ten Plagues
Trust

Some six hundred thousand men and women, not counting their children,[20] then joyfully departed from Egypt, taking with them their livestock and possessions—finally freed from the misery of their bondage to find a new life in the Promised Land.

We are promptly drawn to reflect upon these current times of our twenty-first century where the world is gradually being enslaved by a powerful Socialist movement[21] operated by wealthy globalists determined to establish a new world order based on the kingship of man rather than the Kingship of Christ—and, like Pharaoh, are inflicting persecution on all God's people (especially those beholden to the traditional Faith that Jesus Christ instituted upon the earth).

Yet God's faithful must never give up the fight. Looking back on Moses' unwavering *trust* in the Almighty, it is easy to see that even in the face of a divine chastisement on the ungodly, the Lord God will protect all those who remain obedient to His holy Word.

---

[20] Land of Chanaan, promised by God to Abraham's heirs (Genesis 12:5-7; 13:14-15; Exodus 6:3-5).

[21] Something the Blessed Virgin Mary warned would happen were Russia not consecrated to her Immaculate Heart (her prophetic warning provided to the well-known visionary Sr. Lúcia Santos at Fatima on July 13, 1917) which failure would result in Communist Russia spreading her errors throughout the world.

Chapter 4
EXODUS FROM EGYPT
Patience

Having ascertained the power of Almighty God and the need to obey His every command, we now picture the multitude of Israelites—men, women and children, either on foot or riding on horses, donkeys, mules and camels, steering their herds of cattle, sheep and goats as they make their way through the wilderness, all the while singing songs of praise and thanksgiving to Almighty God as they follow Moses, chosen to shepherd God's flock away from the cruel tyranny of Pharaoh toward the Promised Land, each one filled with the joy of their newfound freedom.

And God called upon the Israelites to keep this time of their exodus as a memorial[1] by celebrating it as a special feast for seven days (under specific guidelines which the Lord provided to Moses)—becoming known as the Feast of the Pasch.[2] Furthermore, God made a covenant with the Israelites that all of their firstborn male children were to be consecrated to the Lord God,[3] and every firstborn of their beasts offered by way of a sacrifice to thank the Almighty for His having freed them from their slavery.

As we follow the Israelites' exodus we learn that the Lord God went before them, guiding their way by a pillar of cloud

---

[1] Exodus 12:14-27.

[2] Feast of the Pasch—sometimes referred to in the Gospels as the Azymes, meaning Feast of Unleavened Bread (Matt. 26:17; Mark 14:1; Acts 12:3; 20:6). Hence Jesus made use of unleavened bread in His institution of the Holy Eucharist at the Last Supper which occurred on the eve of the Pasch (Matt. 26:26; Mark 14:22; Luke 22:19).

[3] Exodus 13:2. Hence we see Mary and Joseph presenting the baby Jesus to His heavenly Father in the Temple of Jerusalem on the fortieth day after His birth (Luke 2:22).

during the day and a pillar of fire at night,[4] thereby enabling the Israelites to continue their journey uninterrupted. In due time, they reached the Red Sea, whereupon God told Moses to have His people set up camp along its shoreline, that they may rest for a while—at the same time revealing to His chosen shepherd[5] that Pharaoh would renege on his earlier agreement to release the Israelites and would seek to pursue them. Even so, God assured Moses that He would remain with His people and would protect them from their evil pursuer and keep them safe. Indeed, before their very eyes, He would deliver due punishment to the rebellious king.

Back in the land of Egypt, just as God had predicted, with all the Israelites gone, Pharaoh all too quickly regretted his having released his slaves, for he now had no more free labor. He hastily gathered together his army with their horses and chariots, determined to find and capture the Israelites and bring them back to Egypt to complete his important storehouses that would hold all of his treasures for himself and his consorts. Some six hundred the king now took with him. With all due speed they charged across the land, his charioteers beating their horses to hasten their pace. Before too long they spotted the Israelites in the far distance camped alongside the vast waters.

At the same time, the Israelites perceived a great cloud of dust on the horizon, heralding Pharaoh's army bearing down upon them, its size like nothing they had ever seen before. With great fear they cried out to their Lord God—while complaining to Moses that he had led their people into the jaws of death, as

---

[4] Exodus 13:21-22.

[5] Exodus 14:4-15.

Exodus from Egypt
Patience

they were now hemmed in between Pharaoh's army and the unsurpassable ocean. But Moses, undeterred in his great faith, called out to the people:

"Fear not: stand and see the great wonders of the Lord, which He will do this day. For the Egyptians whom you see now, you shall see no more for ever."

Even as Moses spoke, God sent down a column of cloud between the Egyptians and the Israelites; one that gave light to the side of God's people and darkness over the oncoming evil.

Then God told Moses to stretch forth his rod over the waters,[6] whereupon a strong, burning wind blew throughout the night. When the Israelites awoke the next morning, to their amazement they perceived the vast waters of the sea now parted—leaving a wide dry pathway between two immense columns of water! Hastily gathering together their families, bundles and animals, the Israelites quickly passed through the gap. Only after they had safely reached the other side did God lift the cloud obscuring the Egyptians' view of what was going on.

Seeing the Israelites on the far side, Pharaoh led his army with full speed ahead—and on reaching the open passage, his charioteers eagerly charged forward determined to reach their target. However, before they could reach the Israelites, God had Moses stretch forth his rod over the waters, which promptly caused the heavy walls to collapse. With a loud thundering noise, the mighty waters crashed over Pharaoh and his army, tossing them around in the turmoil of the waves—killing each and every one of them. Not a single

---

[6] Exodus 14:16-31.

Exodus from Egypt
Patience

Egyptian survived. Dumbstruck, the Israelites stared in awe at what they beheld. As the dead bodies washed up on the far bank, they now respectfully feared the Lord God, humbly acknowledging His great power.

Filled with joy, the multitudes then set forth on the next leg of their journey,[7] singing praises and thanksgiving to Almighty God—led by a canticle introduced by Miriam[8] (sister of Moses and Aaron who was deemed by some as a prophetess) commencing with the words:

"Let us sing to the Lord, for He is gloriously magnified; the horse and his rider He hath thrown into the sea."

Alas it has to be said that as we continue to follow the Israelites' exodus,[9] it appears that the subtle snake of evil had somehow slithered into their presence, provoking fear and discontent to replace their faith-filled gratitude. For having passed through the desert area of Sur where they could find no water, and having then progressed to a place called Mara where the waters were too bitter to drink—instead of praying to the Lord God, the Israelites turned on Moses and blamed him for bringing them to a place where they would now die of thirst. Calling out to His patient Father in Heaven, Moses begged His help—and in response, God showed His faithful servant a tree, which, when Moses cast its branches into the waters, promptly gave them a sweetened flavor.

---

[7] Exodus 15:20-21.

[8] Referred to as Mary in the Douay-Rheims.

[9] Exodus 15:22-25.

Exodus from Egypt
Patience

Lifting his voice to address the people, Moses then told them firmly[10] that if they would have faith in the Lord God, turn to Him for guidance and help, obey His holy Word, they could look forward to a good life, one far removed from that which they had endured in Egypt—valuable words of advice not only for the Israelites but for all of God's faithful children.

Somewhat chastened and imbued with a renewed spirit of determination,[11] the people pressed onward, whereupon they came upon a beautiful place called Elim, with twelve fountains of water and seventy palm trees, everywhere lush and green. Expressing their joyful gratitude, they happily camped here for a few days before continuing their journey.

Nonetheless, as previously noted, in spite of their having witnessed God's great goodness and mercy, whenever the Israelites were faced with a fresh challenge, the snake of discontent, ingratitude and faithlessness would creep into their souls, causing them to complain most bitterly. One example may be seen on the fifteenth day of the second month after the Israelites' exit from Egypt, when their journey led them to an area called Sin,[12] which offered not much by way of food. Once again, instead of praying to God and trusting that He would respond to their prayers, the people complained to Moses and blamed him for having led them here to die of hunger and misery; their complaints accompanied by faithless tears.

So Moses again begged God's mercy and aid, and in response, the Lord told His faithful servant to have Aaron help

---

[10] Exodus 15:26.

[11] Exodus 15:27.

[12] Exodus 16:1-8.

to gather the people together that they may look out across the wilderness, where a large cloud appeared. And Moses told the people that this cloud represented God's glory for He had heard their murmurings and would provide them with food.

Sure enough, that very evening, God sent down a large number of quail[13] which descended over the Israelites' camp providing food for their meal every evening—and in the morning, curtains of dew covered the area, which they could prepare as bread to sustain them throughout the day, for it tasted like flour with honey (*manna*[14] the people called it). Every six days they awoke to find the manna,[15] but as God rested on the seventh, no manna could be found on that day and the people were told to gather sufficient the previous day to tide them over into the Sabbath. Furthermore, at God's command, Moses told Aaron to keep a piece of the manna-bread in a tabernacle as a memorial of God's mercy in keeping His people fed. (Indeed, the manna sustained the Israelites throughout the time of their exodus as they journeyed toward the borders of Chanaan, the Promised Land of 'milk and honey'.)

After leaving the desert area of Sin, the Israelites next arrived in a place called Raphidim on the other side of Mount Sinai (where God had spoken to Moses through the flame of a burning bush)—which provided no water.[16] As what happens when the soul loses faith and the snake of despair creeps in, the Israelites yet again complained to Moses telling him:

---

[13] Quail—collective name for several types of fairly large birds.

[14] Wisdom 16:20-21; Numbers 11:6-9.

[15] Sabbath—Jewish day of rest, being the seventh day of their week.

[16] Exodus 17:1-16.

Exodus from Egypt
Patience

"Why didst thou make us go forth out of Egypt, to kill us and our children, and our beasts with thirst?"

And they even questioned as to whether God was with them. So Moses patiently turned to the Almighty, and in response, was told to take some of the ancients with him and with his rod, was to strike a particular rock on the side of the mountain. Having done as God had instructed, water gushed forth providing the people with fresh water to drink.

Given that their faith was precariously flimsy, the merciful Lord God then showed His people a further miracle to convince them that He was still with them. This new miracle followed the appearance of the warring Amalac tribe who came into the area and attacked the Israelites. Leaving his faithful minister Joshua[17] to lead his people in their defense against the enemy, in accordance with God's instructions Moses took Aaron and another named Hur with him, and standing on the top of a hill, stood with his arms outstretched. As long as he kept his arms extended, the Israelites were able to defeat the Amalacs. Whenever Moses' arms grew heavy and weary, Aaron and Hur helped him to keep his arms upright—and eventually, the enemy took flight. Moses then built an altar here in Raphidim in thanksgiving to Almighty God.

In reviewing the Israelites' exodus thus far, one cannot help but admire the *patience* of Moses in the face of the Israelites' incessant complaining (and even their blaming him each time something went wrong).

---

[17] Named Josue in the Douay-Rheims—son of Nun (Exodus 33:11); a young man whom Moses had appointed as his minister (Numbers 11:28; Deut. 1:38; Josue [Joshua] 1:1).

Exodus from Egypt
Patience

Even more so are we drawn to marvel over the great tolerance of Almighty God, patiently bearing with His people in spite of their faithless ways (as similarly seen in our world today).

Chapter 5
GOD'S HOLY MOUNTAIN
Wisdom

While the Israelites were still camped at Raphidim, which bordered the land of the Madianites, we learn[1] that when Jethro received word that Moses had brought the Israelites into the neighboring area, he promptly set forth to meet his beloved kinsman.

And as at some point Moses had sent his wife and sons back to Jethro during his lengthy stay in Egypt, Jethro now appeared with Sephora, Gersam and Eliezer. We can imagine the family's great rejoicing to be reunited at last.

Taking Jethro aside, Moses then shared with his father-in-law all that had passed between himself and Pharaoh. The priest of Madian listened intently, interested in all that he heard. Giving thanks to Almighty God, he told Moses:

"Blessed is the Lord, who hath delivered you out of the hand of Pharao[h], and out of the hand of the Egyptians."

Thereafter, Jethro and Moses offered up sacrificial holocausts by way of giving praise and further thanksgiving—joined by Aaron and all the ancients, and they ate bread together before the Lord God.

Now in these times, many of God's people would come to Moses, seeking his advice[2]—for they had readily perceived that their strong leader was in fact extremely wise, God having blessed him with the gift of heavenly wisdom. Jethro watched

---

[1] Exodus 18:1-12.

[2] Exodus 18:13-27.

as the people would come to Moses throughout the day and the night, and being a priest himself, he suggested that Moses appoint just and holy men to divide his work among them, depending on their ability to address the various concerns of the people, with the most important and final decisions being left to Moses. God's humble servant listened to his father-in-law's good advice and did all that he suggested. After that, Jethro left Moses and returned to his family, the Madianites.

In the third month after the Israelites' departure from Egypt, we next learn[3] that Moses shepherded God's people out of Raphidim into the neighboring Sinai desert, where they then set up camp near the base of Mount Sinai. Thus God's people were now near the very place where God first spoke to Moses through the flame of a burning bush.

On the Israelites' arrival, the Lord God summoned Moses to come and converse with Him on the mountain top. With a joyful heart, Moses promptly obeyed—while the people looked on, wondering where their leader was going as he climbed the rocky slopes and disappeared out of sight. We pause here to look back on all that Moses had endured to date and how much God loved His wise and faithful servant. Indeed, it may be seen[4] that, unlike those to whom God would speak in a vision, the Lord would communicate directly with Moses, as if one-on-one with a good friend.

Once Moses reached the summit, God gave His faithful servant an important message to convey to the Israelites[5]—that

---

[3] Exodus 19:1-3.

[4] Numbers 12:7-8.

[5] Exodus 19:3-8.

if they would agree to listen to God's holy Word and obey His commandments, He would bless them in a very special way, and they would remain His people, a holy nation, a priestly kingdom[6] for all of their days—words to further inspire all God's faithful to remain strong in the faith and determined to stand firm in the defense of God's holy Word.

In haste, armed with God's message, Moses climbed down the rocky slopes, and having arrived back at the camp, he summoned together the elders and people. After pointing out all that God had done for them in bringing them out of Egypt and carrying them on the *wings of eagles* throughout their many trials, Moses told them of God's new covenant—to which, with one accord, the Israelites agreed, saying:

"All that the Lord hath spoken, we will do."

Moses then returned back up the mountain and after conveying the people's promise to hear God's Word and obey Him,[7] the Almighty told His faithful servant:

"Lo, now will I come to thee in the darkness of a cloud, that the people may hear me speaking to thee, and may believe thee for ever."

In order that the people make ready for this most holy and wondrous event, God sent Moses back down the mountain with instructions that after he had sanctified them, the people were to wash all their clothing, and were to be careful to maintain chastity so that when the Lord God appeared on the third day, they would be suitably prepared. (These valuable words call to mind our own need to keep our souls sanctified

---

[6] Hence the sacred scriptures reveal that Jesus Christ, our Savior and Redeemer, was born of the Jewish House of King David.

[7] Exodus 19:9-15.

at all times in preparation for the unexpected moment of death, at which time we will come before the Lord God and be faced with divine judgement.)

Furthermore, Moses told them that they were not to climb Mount Sinai for it was now God's 'Holy Mountain', and he set boundaries around its base, warning the Israelites that if any should pass these limits, God would punish their disobedience with death. In light of the Israelites having witnessed what happened to the disobedient Pharaoh and his army when charging across the dry pathway dividing the great waters of the Red Sea, we can imagine the people's determination to be obedient to the powerful Lord God—plus they were no doubt somewhat nervous not knowing what to expect when the Almighty would make His appearance. After Moses had sanctified them, they promptly set to work to prepare themselves in accordance with God's instructions.

Very early on the morning of the third day,[8] the Israelites were awoken by the sound of loud crashing thunder. As they fearfully looked up at the mountain from whence came the noise, they perceived its upper echelons enshrouded in a very dark cloud, opened up at regular intervals by flashes of brilliant lightning. Furthermore, the sound of a mighty trumpet filled the air, causing the people to tremble. However, Moses summoned everyone together, telling them that they had no need to fear God—so long as they remained obedient to His holy Word. (These words yet again worth remembering in these current times when attempts are being made to vilify God's Commandments to appease the dictates of sinful man.)

---

[8] Exodus 19:16-17.

Exodus 19:16

God's Holy Mountain
Wisdom

And Moses encouraged the people to stand closer to the base of the mountain—that they may witness the presence of God and believe that the Almighty was truly conversing with him. The people then watched in awe as their leader fearlessly climbed back up the mountain. As Moses disappeared from sight, the sound of the trumpet grew by degrees, louder and louder,[1] its trumpeting blast now drawn out in greater length.

Furthermore, the dark cloud covering the upper echelons turned into a thick smoky haze, fearsome in its awesome density and smelling strongly as of something burning. Indeed, the biblical texts[2] reveal that:

"The Lord was come down upon it in fire, and the smoke arose from it as out of a furnace: and all the Mount was terrible."

We can imagine a sense of panic engulfing the Israelites in their knowledge that the Almighty was conversing with their leader atop the fiery mountain. A short while later—their eyes never leaving the fearsome sight—the people suddenly spotted their shepherd making his way back down the rocky slopes. As they gathered around him, anxious to hear his every word, Moses firmly cautioned them that Almighty God wanted to ensure that none would climb His Holy Mountain—only Moses and those whom God permitted, for it was of course now a most sacred place. And if any were to disobey this commandment, Moses once again warned them that God would be very angry. The people listened in great fear and with one accord assured their leader that all would obey.

---

[1] Exodus 19:19.

[2] Exodus 19:18.

God's Holy Mountain
Wisdom

So Moses returned up the mountain to hear more of God's holy Word, whereupon on reaching the summit[3] the Almighty provided His faithful servant with His famous Ten Commandments and various other laws—which (may our enslaved world of today again take note) if the people obeyed, God promised He would look after them and keep them safe.

Filled with God's holy words of *wisdom*, Moses descended the rocky slopes to reveal all to the people that God had told him.

---

[3] Exodus: Chapters 20, 21, 22, 23.

Exodus 31:18

Chapter 6
TEN COMMANDMENTS
Obedience

In light of all that the Israelites had witnessed, as Moses descended the slopes toward them, every eye was eagerly trained on him, anxious as they were to hear his every word. Finding himself a high spot at the base of the mountain, Moses looked across at their upturned faces, and with a firm voice cautioned them to listen carefully—for God was calling on them to hear and obey everything that he was about to convey to them.

First Moses shared with the people[1] God's holy Ten Commandments, all of which were to be honored and obeyed—not only by the Israelites, but by all God's people for all time (may our disobedient world of today take note). Raising his voice to ensure everyone in his audience could hear, Moses gave them God's First Commandment:

"I am the Lord thy God, who brought thee out of the land of Egypt, out of the house of bondage. Thou shalt not have strange gods before me. Thou shalt not make to thyself a graven thing,[2] nor the likeness of any thing that is in Heaven above, or in the earth beneath, nor of those things that are in the waters under the earth. Thou shalt not adore them, nor serve them."

He then went on to carefully outline God's nine other Commandments, as follows:

---

[1] Exodus 20:1-17.

[2] Graven thing—all carved idols made to be adored and worshipped. On the other hand pictures, statues, or representations (not adored but serving only as a holy reminder) are permitted by God.

Ten Commandments
Obedience

*"Thou shalt not take the name of the Lord thy God in vain...
Remember that thou keep holy the sabbath day... Honour thy father
and thy mother... Thou shalt not kill. Thou shalt not commit
adultery. Thou shalt not steal. Thou shalt not bear false witness
against thy neighbour. Thou shalt not covet thy neighbour's house:
neither shalt thou desire his wife, nor his servant, nor his handmaid,
nor his ox, nor his ass, nor any thing that is his."*

Moses also told the Israelites that God had provided him
with further laws,[3] expounding upon these Ten
Commandments, which he would write down in a book for
their guidance and understanding.

And true to his word, later that same day God's faithful
servant did as he had promised, calling it the 'Book of the
Covenant'. The following morning Moses arose early,[4] and
with the people's help built an altar at the foot of God's Holy
Mountain, which he surrounded with twelve pillars
representing the twelve tribes of Israel. Calling all the people
together, he offered up sacrificial holocausts to Almighty God,
and sprinkled some of the blood of the sacrificed calves over
the altar, keeping the remainder of the blood in a bowl. Then
he read out to the Israelites his written Book of the
Covenant—all of which laws therein the people solemnly
avowed they would obey. At this, Moses sprinkled the blood
over the people, saying:

*"This is the blood of the covenant which the Lord hath made
with you concerning all these words."*

---

[3] Exodus: Chapters 21-23.

[4] Exodus 24:4-8.

Ten Commandments
Obedience

Now in light of the ancients' belief that it is not possible for anyone to actually see God without being smitten with death, to ensure that they remain obedient and believe in Moses, we next learn[5] that God called upon His faithful servant to allow Aaron, his two eldest sons Nadab and Abiu, and seventy of the ancients to accompany him up the mountain. As the group climbed the rocky slopes, about half-way up they were suddenly blessed to see before them a large sparkling sapphire stone, its shining rays extending upwards to create a brilliant light, enshrouding a vision of Almighty God in radiant splendor. We can imagine Aaron, his sons and the seventy ancients filled with awe—not only over this incredibly awesome spectacle but also over the fact that God did not smite them with death. As they quietly descended God's Holy Mountain, no doubt each of them too overwhelmed for speech, their belief in all that Moses had been telling them would have been promptly strengthened.

Next, God spoke to Moses[6] to come again to the mountain top as He wanted to give His faithful servant some further instructions to pass on to the people. At this time, God told Moses that He would provide him with two tablets of stone upon which would be inscribed the Ten Commandments that He had already verbally conveyed to His faithful servant. Believing that he would be gone a long time, Moses assigned Aaron and Hur to look after the people, so that they would have two good men to whom they could address any concerns they may have.

---

[5] Exodus 24:9-10.

[6] Exodus 24:12-15.

Ten Commandments
Obedience

Taking only Joshua with him (his trustworthy young minister who had earlier led the battle against the Amalacs) Moses ascended God's Holy Mountain, the summit of which remained covered with the thick smoky cloud. Leaving Joshua some distance away, Moses disappeared into the burning fire enshrouding the upper echelons, where he remained out of sight for a whole six days. On the seventh day,[7] that the people (and Joshua) may know that God was still speaking with him, the cloud suddenly lifted to reveal Moses standing atop the fiery mountain. The dense smoky haze then reappeared in all its awesome density, removing their leader from their sight while he continued conversing with Almighty God.

This time, Moses was gone for forty days and nights,[8] during which time God provided His faithful servant with careful instructions on what would be needed in order for His holy presence to accompany them on their travels to the Promised Land. And before Moses left his divine Teacher, God gave to His faithful servant the two tablets of stone—upon which were inscribed the Ten Commandments written with the Finger of Almighty God.

Thus armed with God's heavenly gift for our all-time *obedience* to its sacred precepts, Moses returned to Joshua, and the two of them began their descent down God's Holy Mountain.

---

[7] Exodus 24:16-17.

[8] Exodus 24:18; Chapters 25-31:18.

Chapter 7
DIVINE PUNISHMENT
Remorse

As Moses and Joshua drew closer to the Israelites' camp, Joshua remarked that he could hear shouting[1] as though there was some kind of battle in progress. But Moses responded that it was the sound of drunken revelry—for after giving Moses the stone tablets, God had revealed to His faithful servant:[2]

"Go, get thee down: thy people, which thou hast brought out of the land of Egypt, hath sinned. They have quickly strayed from the way which thou didst shew them: and they have made to themselves a molten calf, and have adored it, and sacrificing victims to it, have said: 'These are thy gods, O Israel, that have brought thee out of the land of Egypt'."

Indeed, as Moses had been gone a whole forty days and nights, the people in their typically faithless way[3] had complained to Aaron:

"Arise, make us gods, that may go before us: for as to this Moses, the man that brought us out of the land of Egypt, we know not what has befallen him."

Perhaps believing that his brother had died on the mountain, Aaron too appears to have lost faith. Ignoring God's specific First Commandment that graven idols were not to be adored as gods—in response to the people's persistence, Aaron had them bring various pieces of gold jewelry and ornaments, which he then had melted down and made into a large molten

---

[1] Exodus 32:17-18.

[2] Exodus 32:7-8.

[3] Exodus 32:1-6.

calf. The following morning the people offered up holocausts and adored the idol—and having permitted the devil to take control of their lives, they ate and drank and made drunken merriment. Now after God had revealed to Moses the grievous sin of their idolatry, He shared with His faithful servant that He would have to deal with these stubborn, stiff-necked people,[4] saying:

"Let me alone, that my wrath may be kindled against them, and that I may destroy them, and I will make of thee a great nation."

However, Moses had courageously pleaded with God, begging that He not destroy His people after all that He had done to bring them out of Egypt. In His infinite mercy, God then gave them an opportunity to repent—but to all those who remained stiff-necked in their idolatrous ways, Moses was to punish according to God's instructions.

Returning to Moses and Joshua's descent down God's Holy Mountain, as they approached the camp—in spite of the Almighty having shared with His faithful servant what the Israelites had done—they were both shocked to observe the large golden calf atop the altar that Moses had previously created for the honor of God, with the people making merriment and adoring the graven idol now sacrilegiously adorning it. Deeply mortified by what he beheld, Moses' fiery spirit, tamed over the years, was promptly sparked by the people having broken the First Commandment of Almighty God. In a fit of anger, before he could stop himself, he hurled

---

[4] Exodus 32:10-14.

down the tablets of stone[5]—which instantly broke into pieces and became scattered among the rocks.

As the Israelites looked on in wide-eyed amazement to perceive their shepherd alive and well, Moses promptly set a fire blazing beneath their graven idol,[6] and taking a hammer to what was left of it, he beat the remainder into a pulp. Turning to his brother Aaron, Moses demanded of him:

"What has this people done to thee, that thou shouldst bring upon them a most heinous sin?"

But Aaron could find no plausible response—clearly, he and all those who were with him had lost faith, and having stripped themselves of God's grace, had given in to the people's demands. We next see Moses summoning the masses,[7] and standing before them—knowing that due punishment was needed to appease the wrath of Almighty God—he called out to them:

"If any man be on the Lord's side let him join with me."

All the sons of Levi[8] (including Aaron and his sons Nadab and Abiu) gathered around Moses, deeply mortified, humbly professing their belief and support. In accordance with God's instructions, Moses then ordered them to go forth throughout the camp and slay every idolater who wished to remain caught up in this evil of worshipping idols. Some three and twenty thousand idolaters were slain that day—their punishment

---

[5] Exodus 32:19.

[6] Exodus 32:20-25.

[7] Exodus 32:26-28.

[8] Sons of Levi—one of the tribes of Israel, traditionally descended from Levi, son of Jacob; they served particular religious duties for the Israelites and had political responsibilities as well.

emphasizing the need to obey God's First Commandment out of love and respect for the Almighty, creator of the universe and all that is contained therein.

As we reflect upon the Israelites' disobedience, we are drawn to recall a similar idolatrous event that occurred in the twentieth century when the ruling Pontiff[9] (for the first time in the history of the Church) permitted a pagan idol to be placed atop the holy Tabernacle in the Basilica of St. Francis of Assisi, Italy (October 27, 1986) and adored by idolaters like Animists and Voodoo worshippers—who the Pope had invited to join him and people of all faiths and religions in what he called a 'World Day of Prayer for Peace'. That we be not mistaken, when an earthquake hit Central Italy on September 26, 1997, it caused the roof of that same Basilica to cave in directly over the most sacred altar, desecrated as it was by that sacrilegious act of 1986. As seen throughout the Scriptures, having given time for due repentance and receiving none, God never fails to show where error is in need of correction.

In pondering on the justice of our divine Teacher, we are drawn to wonder what lies in store for our disobedient world of today in light of a number of other such similar events being permitted (once again, breaking God's First Commandment). To cite just one example, on October 4, 2020 the current Pontiff[10] allowed a pagan Pachamama idol to be adored and worshipped in the Vatican Gardens, and on October 7, 2020

---

[9] Pope John Paul II (born Karol Józef Wojtyła), Polish (May 18, 1920-Apr. 2, 2005); Pope from Oct. 16, 1978 until his death.

[10] Pope Francis (born Jorge Mario Bergoglio, Dec. 17, 1936); first Jesuit pope, Argentinian; elected to the papacy, March 13, 2013.

went further to place the idol in front of the main altar of St. Peter's Basilica in Rome.

Returning now to the story of Moses, God's faithful shepherd addressed the people,[11] telling them that as they had committed this very grave sin but were now filled with remorse, he would ascend God's Holy Mountain and plead with the Almighty that He forgive them for their terrible trespass against His First Commandment. While the people waited in trepidation, Moses went back up into the dark cloud and pleaded with the Lord God on their behalf:

"I beseech Thee: this people hath sinned a heinous sin, and they have made to themselves gods of gold: either forgive them this trespass, or if Thou do not, strike me out of the book[12] that Thou hast written."

In response God told His faithful servant:

"He that hath sinned against me, him will I strike out of my book: But go thou, and lead this people whither I have told thee: my angel shall go before thee."

By this, we learn that God would no longer be journeying with the Israelites[13] lest He become angry over their faithless, stiff-necked ways, and justifiably exterminate them (yet again, valuable words for our fallen world of today to keep in mind). When the people heard these bad tidings, they were even more mortified. By way of penance, they laid aside their ornaments (which the Israelites were prone to wear in abundance) and in

---

[11] Exodus 32:30-35.

[12] Book—meaning *the book of life*, a figurative catalogue of the names of all those destined to enjoy Everlasting Life (Exodus 32:32; Psalms 68:29; 138:16; Phil. 4:3; Eccl. [Sirach] 24:32; Apoc. [Rev.] 3:5; 13:8; 17:8; 20:12; 20:15; 21:27).

[13] Exodus 33:2-11.

accordance with God's instructions laid them at the foot of His Holy Mountain.

At the same time, Moses took the sacred piece of manna and his Book of the Covenant and removed them from the people's midst—and pitching a tent outside of the camp, he placed them within, calling the tent the 'Tabernacle of the Covenant'. No longer did Moses meet with his divine Master on the top of Mount Sinai; instead, whenever God wished to converse with him, He would appear in a pillar of cloud, hovering over the entrance of the sacred tent.

As soon as the people saw the cloud, from their place within the camp, they would bow down and worship their Lord God—each of them still filled with remorse over their having broken His First Commandment. Whenever the cloud was absent, the people would come to the entrance of the sacred tent, and humbly seek the advice of their trustworthy shepherd; and on those occasions when Moses had need to return to the camp, he would leave Joshua inside the Tabernacle, where his faithful minister would remain until his return.

We next learn[14] that before the people left Mount Sinai to continue their journey to the Promised Land, Moses pleaded with his Heavenly Father that His holy presence may be with them during their travels:

"For how shall we be able to know, I and Thy people, that we have found grace in Thy sight, unless Thou walk with us."

At this, in His great mercy God assured Moses that He would consider his request:

---

[14] Exodus 33:12-23.

Exodus 32:4-6

Divine Punishment
Remorse

"For thou hast found grace before me, and thee I have known by name."

We can imagine these words filling Moses with a profound sense of closeness to his Heavenly Father. Looking up into the cloud, he humbly begged that he might see God's holy Face—whereupon the Almighty gently responded:

"Thou canst not see my Face: for man shall not see me and live."

It would seem indeed from an interpretation of these words found in the notes of the Douay-Rheims Bible that the Lord God usually spoke to Moses in the pillar of a cloud so that he did not see God's full glory, albeit the Lord would speak familiarly with Moses as with a friend. The interpretation goes further to explain that through such a vision Moses was allowed to see something of God in an assumed corporeal form—but not His holy Face, the rays of which would be too bright for the human eye to bear.

After their intimate dialogue, God instructed Moses[1] to create two stone tablets like the ones that he had smashed, and the following morning was to ascend Mount Sinai bringing the new tablets with him—there to meet the Almighty on the summit of His Holy Mountain for the last time. And once again, Moses was to ensure that none would follow him up the slopes. So very early the next morning, Moses dutifully obeyed, taking with him two new tablets of stone. On reaching the summit, God came down in a cloud, whereupon Moses humbly greeted his Heavenly Father:

"O the Lord, the Lord God, merciful and gracious, patient and of much compassion, and true, who keepest mercy unto thousands,

---

[1] Exodus 34:1-11.

who takest away iniquity, and wickedness, and sin, and no man of himself is innocent before thee. Who renderest the iniquity of the fathers to the children, and to the grandchildren, unto the third and fourth generation."

And prostrating himself upon the ground, Moses then pleaded with the Almighty:

"If I have found grace in Thy sight: O Lord, I beseech Thee, that Thou wilt go with us (for it is a stiff-necked people) and take away our iniquities and sin, and possess us."

No doubt much to Moses' joy, God now responded that, providing the people obeyed all of His Ten Commandments and laws, He would journey with them and would grant them many signs and wonders, that the people may know that their Lord God was with them, helping them to conquer the idolatrous Amorrhites, Chanaanites, Hethites, Pherezites, Hevites, Jebusites, who were occupying the land promised to the Israelites' forefathers Abraham, Isaac and Jacob.[2] At the same time, the Lord God warned His faithful servant:[3]

"Beware thou never join in friendship with the inhabitants of that land, which may be thy ruin. But destroy their altars, break their statues, and cut down their groves.[4] Adore not any strange god… Make no covenant with the men of those countries lest, when they have committed fornication with their gods, and have adored their idols, some one call thee to eat of the things sacrificed." (Yet again, valuable words for our fallen world to hearken and obey.)

---

[2] Exodus 33:1.

[3] Exodus 34:12-15.

[4] *Groves*—places chosen for idolatrous worship (Exodus 34:13; Deut. 7:5; 12:3).

Divine Punishment
Remorse

Now on this occasion,[5] Moses was gone yet another forty days and nights as the Almighty continued to teach His faithful servant. Throughout this time, deeply mortified over his kinsmen having broken God's First Commandment, Moses fasted by way of making reparation to his beloved Lord God for the Israelites' idolatrous sinfulness. When finally Moses descended the mountain armed with the new tablets of stone upon which God had written His Ten Commandments, we learn[6] that Aaron and the elders were much disturbed, as the face of their shepherd now shone like the rays of the sun—such that they were afraid to go near him, feeling further great shame over their earlier disobedience. Indeed, Moses had to cover his face whenever he spoke with them.

Dear Moses, albeit he had done no wrong, out of his determined efforts to lead his flock down the paths of righteousness, took upon himself to make reparation for their sinful disobedience—his noble fasting perhaps the reason for God's shining light illuminating his countenance.

Looking back to these times and comparing them with our modern sinful world, it seems pertinent to pause for a moment to reflect upon the virtue of true *remorse* and the infinite mercy of God when He perceives a truly repentant heart.

---

[5] Exodus 34:17-28.

[6] Exodus 34:29-35.

Chapter 8
TABERNACLE OF THE COVENANT
Holiness

In light of the Israelites' renewed faithfulness, and in accordance with God's earlier instructions provided to Moses the first time he was gone for forty days and nights, God's faithful servant now summoned the people and revealed to them all that the Lord God was requiring of them,[1] that His holy presence may be with them during their travels to the Promised Land.

First, they would need to make a sacred chest (the 'Ark of the Testimony') which was to become the portable earthly dwelling place of God's holy presence, and within which would be carried the two stone tablets of God's Ten Commandments and the piece of manna. Furthermore, a sacred tent (the 'Tabernacle of the Covenant') was to be made of wood, capable of being folded down and transported, within which the Ark of the Testimony was to be placed each time the Israelites set up camp.

The people listened intently, anxious to appease their Lord God and abide by all that God's holy messenger was asking of them. In the face of their enthusiasm, Moses took care to remind them of God's Commandment[2] that only six days were the people to work—for God forbade any to work on the seventh (the Sabbath), and any disobedience to that Commandment, Moses warned them, would be met by the wrath of Almighty God.

---

[1] Exodus 35:1-10.

[2] Exodus 35:2.

Exodus 40:1-11

Tabernacle of the Covenant
Holiness

In order to commence work on the sacred project, Moses called upon the people to offer to the Lord God whatever they would be willing to donate[1]—gold, silver, brass; fine linens that had twice been dyed violet, purple and scarlet; goats' hair and the skins of rams dyed red and violet; setim wood;[2] oil to make ointments and to keep the lamps burning; spices to make fragrant incense; onyx stones and other gems to adorn the robe of the high priest (known as the ephod[3] with its embroidered breastplate known as the rational[4]), the high priest to be appointed in due time.

Eager to make atonement for their sinfulness, the people delivered their offerings in abundance. Both men and women donated jewelry and other ornaments of gold, silver and brass; the princes offered onyx and other precious stones for the ephod and its rational; skillful women gave the first fruits of linens that they had spun and twice dyed in the specified colors; others brought spices and oils. Indeed, so generous were their offerings that Moses had to restrain the people from bringing anything more.[5]

To accomplish the intricacies of the work that was required, God appointed two trustworthy craftsman, Beseleel[6] and Ooliab[7] by name, both of whom God had blessed with the

---

[1] Exodus 35:11-29.

[2] Setim wood—so named in the Douay-Rheims; also known as acacia wood.

[3] Ephod—special garment worn only by the high priest.

[4] Rational—piece of embroidery worn on the breast of the high priest and adorned with twelve precious stones representing the twelve tribes of Israel.

[5] Exodus 36:6-7.

[6] Beseleel—son of Uri, son of Hur of the tribe of Juda (Exodus 31:2; 35:30; 36:1; 37:1; 38:22; 2 Paralipomenon [2 Chronicles] 1:5).

[7] Ooliab—son of Achisamech of the tribe of Dan (Exodus 31:6; 35:34; 36:1; 38:23).

necessary knowledge, wisdom and professional skills.[8] Beseleel was to take care of the work needed for the creation of the sacred chest, while Ooliab was entrusted with the portable Tabernacle. Various experts came forward to offer their services to assist with the work.

Turning first to the Ark of the Testimony,[9] this sacred chest was to be made from setim wood, fashioned in accordance with specific dimensions, and overlaid with the purest gold (both within and without), with four gold rings attached to each corner through which would run two carrying poles (also made of setim wood, overlaid with gold) enabling the Ark to be carried by four bearers. The top of the chest was to be crowned with gold, upholding a rectangular slab of solid gold (known as the 'Propitiatory') upon which would rest two gold cherubims affixed to the solid slab and facing each other with their wings spread apart so that both sides of the Propitiatory would be covered.

Turning now to the Tabernacle of the Covenant,[10] its walls were to be constructed from a specified number of boards (similarly made from setim wood and overlaid with gold) designed in accordance with specific measurements, and as previously mentioned, in a way that would enable them to be folded down and transported (ultimately by six covered wagons, each led by a team of two oxen[11]). To ensure stability once erected, gold-plated bars, held up by rings of gold, were to run horizontally along the length of the walls, together with

[8] Exodus 35:30-35; 36:1.

[9] Exodus 25:10-20; 37:1-9.

[10] Exodus 26:15-30; 36:20-38.

[11] Numbers 7:3.

vertically-placed square-shaped pillars, supported by silver sockets at the base of each, positioned at regular intervals.

The end result of the completed Tabernacle would resemble a small temple, being the holy dwelling-place of God—containing the Ark of the Testimony at the far end, separated from the rest of the Tabernacle by a specially designed curtain (known as the 'veil'),[12] thereby creating a sanctuary (called the 'Holy of Holies') for the Ark.

Aside from the veil that would separate the Holy of Holies from the rest of the Tabernacle, other curtains were to be made[13]—not only to line the interior walls of the sacred tent, but also to cover the entrance of the Tabernacle. All of the curtains were to be fashioned from twisted fine linens, twice dyed with the required colors of violet, purple and scarlet, and then embroidered, with rings of gold attached to loops lining the top and sides of the curtaining, accompanied by buckles of brass to fasten them together. Furthermore, heavy covers were to be made to protect the roof of the Tabernacle:[14] eleven to be made of goats' hair, with another single cover made from rams' skins dyed red, and over that another of violet colored skins.

In front of the veil separating the Holy of Holies, an altar[15] was to be placed, upon which incense would be burned[16] and priestly sacrifices offered (referred to as the 'Altar of Incense' or sometimes the 'Altar of Sacrifice') with a brazen grate below

---

[12] Exodus 26:31-33.

[13] Exodus 27:9-18; 36:8-18.

[14] Exodus 26:7, 14.

[15] Exodus 27:1-8; 30:1-5.

[16] The burning of incense being deemed an emblem of prayer, ascending to the Almighty from an inflamed heart (Psalms 140:2; Apoc. 5:8; 8:4).

to contain the required fire for the sacrificial offerings. This altar was also to be constructed from setim wood overlaid with gold, with horns at the four corners, and the usual gold rings attached to each corner through which the gold-plated wooden carrying poles would run, the entire altar fashioned in accordance with specific measurements. Pans were to be made to receive the ashes from the sacrifices, along with tongs, fleshhooks and firepans, all of these vessels to be made of brass.

Close to the Altar of Incense, a table[17] of specific measurements would need to stand (similarly made from gold-plated setim wood, with the usual carrying poles running along either side) upon which was to be placed the twelve loaves of proposition, known as the 'face-bread', so named because they were always to stand before the face of the Lord in the Holy of Holies.[18] And upon the table certain dishes, bowls, censers and cups were to be placed,[19] being sacred vessels for the sacrificial offerings, each to be made from the purest gold.

Beseleel made an intricate stand-alone gold candlestick,[20] capable of holding seven candles: three on either side of a single slightly elevated candle, providing light to the priests when offering their sacrifices in the otherwise darkness of the enclosed Tabernacle (perhaps indicative of the light of the Holy Ghost and His sevenfold grace in the sanctuary of Christ's holy

---

[17] Exodus 25:23-30; 37:10-15.

[18] A pre-figuring of the Eucharistic sacrifice and sacrament in the Church that the Son of God would later institute, replacing this Old Covenant with the New.

[19] Exodus 25:29; 37:16.

[20] Exodus 25:31-39; 37:17-29.

Mother Church). And finally, a large basin[21] (called the 'laver') affixed to a portable stand, was to be fashioned from brass and positioned close to the Altar of Incense—this laver to contain holy water for the priests to cleanse and purify their hands and feet.

It isn't difficult to imagine the hive of activity within the camp, all the people eager to assist Beseleel and Ooliab to prepare whatever was needed. Once all the items had been made, God spoke to Moses[22] telling him that on the first day of the first month of the second year, he was to erect the Tabernacle with all of the curtaining hung in place—and the Ark of the Testimony placed at the far end behind the veil, shutting it off from the rest of the Tabernacle. The Altar of Incense was to be placed in position, along with the table containing the face-bread and sacred vessels. All seven candles in the candlestick holder were to be lit, and the laver filled with water.

Moses was then to take the oil of unction and anoint the Tabernacle with its adornments, to include the Ark, the altar, the table with its sacred vessels, and the laver filled with water—that every item may be appropriately sanctified. He was then to summon the people to gather at the entrance of the Tabernacle[23] so that in their presence, Moses could offer Aaron and his sons Nadab and Abiu as holy priests (that they may minister to the Lord God in an everlasting priesthood).

---

[21] Exodus 30:18.

[22] Exodus 40:1-11.

[23] Exodus 40:12-14.

Tabernacle of the Covenant
Holiness

Having accomplished all in accordance with God's instructions,[24] Moses first washed the hands and feet of Aaron, Nadab and Abiu with the holy water from the laver, and then proceeded to anoint them with the oil of unction; thereafter vesting them with the straight linen garments (fashioned in accordance with God's specific guidelines and girdled about the waist[25]). At the same time, Moses consecrated his brother Aaron as high priest, placing upon him the ephod with its embroidered rational, and setting upon his head a mitre.

God then sent down a cloud over the Tabernacle[26] and the glory of the Almighty filled it. So long as the cloud hung over the Tabernacle the people were to stay encamped—but as soon as God lifted His cloud, the holy tent was to be dismantled so that the people could move on.[27]

Once in transit, during the daytime God would bring down His cloud over the Ark of the Testimony—and at night, a fiery cloud so that the people could see the glory of God shining upon it.[28]

Thus the *holiness* of God's divine presence travelled with His people, keeping them safe in the wilderness as they headed toward the land of 'milk and honey' promised by God to their forefathers Abraham, Isaac and Jacob.

---

[24] Leviticus 8:1-9.

[25] Exodus 28:2-39.

[26] Exodus 40:32.

[27] Exodus 40:34-35.

[28] Exodus 40:36.

Chapter 9
JOURNEY THROUGH THE WILDERNESS
Faithfulness

A s we follow the Israelites' progress, we learn that when Moses would enter the Tabernacle to consult his divine Teacher, he would hear God's voice speaking to him from beneath the wings of the two cherubims[1] covering the Propitiatory of the Ark, when it was set up inside the Holy of Holies at the far end of the sacred tent—thereby providing Moses with guidance throughout the Israelites' journey across the wilderness toward the Promised Land.

To help the people maintain some form of order each time they were to move on, God instructed Moses to have two trumpets of beaten silver made,[2] which were then used to alert the various groups when it was their turn to take their place in the departing columns (which responsibility Moses assigned to Nadab and Abiu).

In visualizing the Israelites' journeying, we picture the Ark being carried on the shoulders of its four priestly bearers by means of its gold-plated poles, followed by the six covered wagons, each drawn by a pair of oxen and carrying the dismantled Tabernacle and its sacred vessels—which wagons and oxen the princes and chiefs of the twelve tribes of Israel had donated[3] (and which Moses placed under the care of the priestly Levites, to whom he also assigned responsibility for transporting the sacred Tabernacle from place to place).

---

1 Numbers 7:89.

[2] Numbers 10:1-8.

[3] Numbers 7:2-9.

Journey Through the Wilderness

Journey Through The Wilderness
Faithfulness

It could not have been an easy journey through the wilderness, for indeed the barren, infertile land offered very little. Even so, in His infinite mercy God continued to provide food for the people—being manna, as previously mentioned.

Now at the time of the Israelites' departure from the wicked Pharaoh in Egypt, a number of others who were not of the race of Israel had joined them.[1] But in light of these people having grown up in the pagan culture of Egypt, as Moses led the travelling caravans deeper into the wilderness, rather than being grateful for the food that the good Lord God had provided, they complained that the manna was nothing like the colorful and tasty fruits that they had left behind in Egypt (things like cucumbers, melons, leeks, onions and even garlic, they said) and they complained bitterly that they had no flesh to eat. To those Israelites around them with whom they had made friends, their influence now goaded them into similarly complaining out loud (this clearly confirming why the Lord God had previously warned the people through Moses that they must avoid associating with the ungodly, lest they be drawn to follow their sinful ways).

To teach all of His weak-willed people a lesson, we learn that God showed His displeasure with all those who had allowed themselves to be influenced by the ungodly—by consuming them with fire (the place of their punishment becoming known as 'the Burning'[2]).

Yet in spite of this divine chastisement, it seems that a number of the Israelites continued to surrender to the snake of

---

[1] Numbers 11:1-6.

[2] Numbers 11:3.

discontent as it quietly slithered amongst them. They now complained non-stop against Moses[3] that they had no flesh to eat—whereupon Moses cried out to his Heavenly Father:

"Whence should I have flesh to give to so great a multitude? They weep against me, saying: Give us flesh that we may eat. I am not able alone to bear all this people, because it is too heavy for me. But if it seem unto Thee otherwise, I beseech Thee to kill me, and let me find grace in Thy eyes, that I be not afflicted with so great evils."

In His infinite mercy, God first comforted His beloved servant, telling him to gather together seventy ancients[4] (possibly the same ancients who had been blessed with the vision of Almighty God on His Holy Mountain) and to bring them to the entrance of the Tabernacle—whereupon God would gift them with holy wisdom to ensure that Moses would no longer bear the burden of the ungrateful, faithless Israelites alone.

As for the people's continual complaints that they had no flesh to eat, we learn[5] that God's wrath was *exceedingly enkindled*—such that He commanded Moses to tell the people:

"Be ye sanctified: tomorrow you shall eat flesh: for I have heard you say: Who will give us flesh to eat? It was well with us in Egypt. That the Lord may give you flesh, and you may eat: Not for one day, nor two, nor five, nor ten, no nor for twenty. But even for a month of days, till it come out at your nostrils, and become loathsome to you,

---

[3] Numbers 11:13-15.

[4] Numbers 11:16. As noted in the Challoner edition of the Douay-Rheims, this was the first institution of the council or senate (the Sanhedrin), consisting of seventy or seventy-two senators or counsellors.

[5] Numbers 11:10; 11:18-20.

because you have cast off the Lord, who is in the midst of you, and have wept before him, saying: Why came we out of Egypt?"

Shortly thereafter, there appeared throughout the camp an abundance of quail.[6] But rather than being grateful to the Lord God for their miraculous appearance, these same people consumed the flesh with gluttonous self-indulgence—whereupon the Almighty punished their faithless ingratitude by allowing their sin of greed to afflict them with a great plague which appears to have struck them down, the place of their burial becoming known as the 'graves of the lust' (so-called from their inordinate desire for flesh).

In pondering on these divine chastisements we are once again drawn to wonder what lies in store for our world of today, where the greed of man to have his own sinful way has resulted in a kingship of man as opposed to the Kingship of Christ.

Returning now to the seventy ancients, after God had gifted them with heavenly wisdom, these newly ordained prophets (so named in the biblical texts[7]) went among the people encouraging them to hear the Word of God (following in the footsteps of Moses, who they still looked upon as their guiding shepherd). At this time, as Miriam[8] (sister of Moses and Aaron) was deemed by some to be a prophetess, she now approached Moses, accompanied by Aaron,[9] and the two of them challenged their brother (regarded as the greatest of all

---

[6] Numbers 11:31-34.

[7] Meaning a person chosen to speak for God and to guide the people of Israel (Challoner edition of the Douay-Rheims).

[8] As previously mentioned, referred to as Mary in the Douay-Rheims.

[9] Numbers 12:1-15.

prophets) as to why God should grant him special favors when surely God favors all of His prophets and prophetesses. In his humble way, Moses refused to defend himself, whereupon the Lord God came down in a pillar of cloud before the entrance of the Tabernacle, summoning Aaron and Miriam to stand before Him. They then heard the Almighty speaking to them:

"Hear my words: if there be among you a prophet of the Lord, I will appear to him in a vision, or I will speak to him in a dream. But it is not so with my servant Moses who is most faithful in all my house: For I speak to him mouth to mouth: and plainly, and not by riddles and figures doth he see the Lord."

And to show His displeasure over their having challenged His faithful prophet, God withdrew His cloud from their sight, and Miriam's skin appeared white as snow for she was now afflicted with leprosy. Seeing their sister thus stricken, Aaron appealed to Moses, confessing the sin that he and Miriam had *foolishly committed* and begging that she be healed. In his usual saintly way, Moses then appealed to the Almighty begging Him to heal their sister—but we note that God told Moses:

"If her Father had spitten upon her face, ought she not to have been ashamed for seven days at least? Let her be separated seven days without the camp, and afterwards she shall be called again."

So the leprosy remained with Miriam for a whole seven days, during which time she had to remain outside of the camp before God granted her a healing and permitted her to return to the Israelites.

Journey Through The Wilderness
Faithfulness

As we continue to follow the Israelites' travels, in due time they reached the desert of Pharan[10] which bordered Chanaan, the Promised Land. Stretching ahead lay hills and plains, valleys and rivers, and in the far distance, cities. The great multitudes stared at what lay before them, wondering how they would fare in this foreign land. So Moses sent forth twelve spies—leaders from each of the twelve tribes of Israel (to include his faithful minister Joshua and another warrior of the faith named Caleb, son of Jephone the Cenezite)—telling them:

"Go you up by the south side. And when you shall come to the mountains, view the land, of what sort it is: and the people that are the inhabitants thereof, whether they be strong or weak: few in number or many: The land itself, whether it be good or bad: what manner of cities, walled or without walls: The ground, fat or barren, woody or without trees. Be of good courage, and bring us of the fruits of the land."

The spies were gone forty days and nights,[11] and on their return, armed with various luscious fruits, told the people that the land indeed *"floweth with milk and honey"*. However, aside from Joshua and Caleb, the spies cast a bleak and frightening picture, reporting that the cities were great and walled, and the inhabitants extremely tall and strong looking, some appearing as giants—inciting fear into all by telling them that an attack would be hopeless as none would survive. We note that Joshua and Caleb on the other hand,[12] were both firm in their faith that the Lord God would keep them all safe, telling the people that

---

[10] Numbers 13:1-21.

[11] Numbers 13:26-30.

[12] Numbers 14:1-12.

they believed they should still go forth and possess the land—for such was the Will of Almighty God. But few would listen to Joshua and Caleb. Instead, they murmured against Moses and Aaron, saying:

"Would God that we had died in Egypt and would God we may die in this vast wilderness, and that the Lord may not bring us into this land, lest we fall by the sword, and our wives and children be led away captives. Is it not better to return into Egypt?"

And they said to one another:

"Let us appoint a captain, and let us return into Egypt."

At this, Joshua and Caleb cried out all the louder, telling the faithless people:

"The land which we have gone round is very good: If the Lord be favourable, He will bring us into it, and give us a land flowing with milk and honey. Be not rebellious against the Lord: and fear ye not the people of this land, for we are able to eat them up as bread. All aid is gone from them: the Lord is with us, fear ye not."

Sadly, their words only served to anger the stiff-necked people—for they had clearly fallen prey to the fear-mongering tactics of those who had not the courage to trust in Almighty God (as similarly seen in our world today). That a valuable lesson may be learned, as the fear-driven, faithless Israelites now sought to stone Joshua and Caleb, the Lord God appeared in a thick cloud over the Tabernacle[13] and told Moses that He would destroy all those who in their fear-driven lack of faith were refusing to accept His holy Will.

---

[13] Numbers 14:20-30.

Journey Through The Wilderness
Faithfulness

Fortunately for the Israelites, Moses appealed to the Almighty, begging Him to forgive the people for their stiff-necked ways—and in His infinite mercy, God once again gave in to His favored prophet's pleas, saying He would not punish them with death. But as just punishment was due—to all who had witnessed God's majesty and all the signs that He had done in Egypt and in the wilderness, and all those spies who had now tempted the people through fear to ignore His holy Word—of these, none would dwell in the land that God had promised to their forefathers.

Instead, they would wander in the desert for forty years, and any attempts to conquer the Promised Land would fail, for their Lord God would no longer be with them. Only Joshua and Caleb, on account of their *faithfulness* in the face of the Israelites' iniquity, would live to conquer the Promised Land.

Deut. 34:1-5

Chapter 10
FORTY YEARS OF PUNISHMENT
Humility

A s we follow the Israelites' forty years of punishment, we are provided with a number of important warnings—over and above those already gleaned during the lifetime of Moses when all those who disobeyed God's holy Word brought upon themselves justly deserved divine punishment.

We note from the biblical texts[1] that a rebellion against the Word of God is born of the sin of pride—prompting the realization that the snake of arrogance is tempting our world today to vilify God's Commandments and other traditional sacred precepts to suit the dictates of sinful man. Yet, as evidenced by the punishment of the Israelites when they broke God's First Commandment, we know that the good Lord God chastises all those who persistently give in to Satan's wiles—as further revealed during these times of the Israelites' forty years in the wilderness when a man was seen breaking the Sabbath Commandment and was stoned to death.[2]

A further lesson may be learned from the divine chastisement that was delivered to three Levi priests named Core, Dathan and Abiron,[3] who had influenced some two hundred and fifty thousand of their congregation to join them in rebelling against the authority that God had assigned to Moses and Aaron. In light of such rebellious behavior, God

---

[1] Numbers 15:30-31.

[2] Numbers 15:32-36.

[3] Numbers 16:1-2.

commanded Moses and Aaron[4] to keep well away from them and all those who were supporting their sinful cause that He *"may presently destroy them."*

But Moses and Aaron beseeched the Lord God to have mercy on all those who had been wrongfully influenced,[5] that they be given a chance to wake up to the truth (their prayerful request somewhat similar to that being conducted in our world today, where prayers are being offered for those who have been influenced to fall away from the true traditional Faith that our Lord and Savior taught to His Twelve Apostles, handed down through the Early Church Fathers and the traditional Mass).

Returning to the story, we learn that God in His infinitely merciful way, gave the people an opportunity to withdraw from their rebellious leaders, telling Moses to command the people to separate themselves from the tents of Core, Dathan and Abiron. In obedience to God's command, Moses went forth, along with Aaron and the seventy ancients, and standing a good distance from where two of the priests (Dathan and Abiron) and their congregation were assembled, Moses called out to the people:

"Depart from the tents of these wicked men, and touch nothing of theirs, lest you be involved in their sins."

Perhaps somewhat fearful, a great number of the congregation poured forth and hurriedly distanced themselves,[6] whereupon Dathan and Abiron appeared at the

---

[4] Numbers 16:20-21.

[5] Numbers 16:22-26.

[6] Numbers 16:27-33.

entrance, along with their families and those who remained in support of them. As they stood there, no doubt somewhat perturbed, they would have heard Moses telling the people:

"By this you shall know that the Lord hath sent me to do all things that you see, and that I have not forged them of my own head: If these men die the common death of men, and if they be visited with a plague, wherewith others also are wont to be visited, the Lord did not send me. But if the Lord do a new thing, and the earth opening her mouth swallow them down, and all things that belong to them, and they go down alive into hell, you shall know that they have blasphemed the Lord."

Immediately after Moses said these words, much to the horror of all those watching, the Lord God opened up the ground at the very feet of the disobedient priests—such that they and their supporters fell into the great abyss and *went down alive into hell* (as the Lord God then closed the ground over them). Furthermore, God brought down fire over Core,[7] the one who had instigated the rebellion, along with all those who had continued to side with him. Even those Israelites who later murmured against Moses and Aaron, accusing them of killing the *people of the Lord*—God punished by destroying them too (some fourteen thousand seven hundred men besides those who had perished in the sedition of Core[8]).

Looking back over these divine punishments, we are once again drawn to ponder on these times of our twenty-first century, where efforts are being made to abrogate the traditional Faith of Christ's holy Mother Church, similarly

---

[7] Numbers 16:5-35.

[8] Numbers 16:49.

creating division among the faithful. Yet even if these divine chastisements be not sufficient to convince all those in priestly authority who are decrying the traditional sacred precepts instituted by Christ, a further warning may be found when the Israelites entered a place called Cades[9] (in a different part of the vast desert to that where the Israelites had previously camped at Raphidim). Once again, the area offered no water.

In their typical way, rather than praying to their good Lord God with patience and faith, the people complained against Moses and Aaron, telling them:

"Why have you made us come up out of Egypt, and have brought us into this wretched place which cannot be sowed, nor bringeth forth figs, nor vines, nor pomegranates, neither is there any water to drink?"

After Moses and Aaron had gone into the sacred Tabernacle and appealed yet again to the Almighty, God told Moses:

"Take the rod, and assemble the people together, thou and Aaron thy brother, and speak to the rock before them, and it shall yield waters. And when thou hast brought forth water out of the rock, all the multitude and their cattle shall drink." (Here, we note that God did not tell Moses to *"strike the rock with his rod"* as He had previously commanded at Raphidim.)

Having assembled the multitudes, his fiery spirit no doubt rekindled over the people's continual ingratitude toward his beloved Lord God, Moses cried out to them:

---

[9] Numbers 20:1-11.

Forty Years of Punishment
Humility

"Hear, ye rebellious and incredulous: Can we bring you forth water out of this rock?"

And instead of *speaking to the rock* as God had commanded, Moses struck the rock twice with his rod[10]—which, while promptly bringing forth an abundance of water, compelled the Almighty to admonish His servant:[11]

"Because you have not believed me, to sanctify me before the children of Israel, you shall not bring these people into the land, which I will give them."

Furthermore, as Aaron in his important role of high priest did not attempt to stop his brother, God advised that he too would not be allowed to enjoy the fruits of the Promised Land.[12] Indeed, the Almighty directed Moses to lead the Israelites to a place at the foot of Mount Hor[13] where He commanded that Moses take Aaron to the mountain top, along with Aaron's youngest son Eleazar[14]—that Aaron be stripped of his priestly vestments which were to be transferred over to Eleazar who, in light of his father being *incredulous to [God's] words at the waters of contradiction,* was to take over his role as the high priest.

---

[10] *"You have not believed"*—meaning, as explained in the Douay-Rheims, that the fault of Moses and Aaron, on this occasion, was a certain diffidence and weakness of faith; not the doubting of God's power or veracity but apprehending the unworthiness of that rebellious and incredulous people, and therefore speaking with some ambiguity.

[11] Numbers 20:12.

[12] Numbers 20:24.

[13] Numbers 20:25-28.

[14] Not to be confused with Moses' son, Eliezer.
Furthermore, we note from Leviticus 10:1-2 that Aaron's two older sons Nadab and Abiu by this time had passed from this life—for they had disobediently offered a sacrifice with 'foreign fire' before the Lord God, and were promptly consumed by the flames.

Forty Years of Punishment
Humility

Having ascended Mount Hor, and Moses having transferred Aaron's priestly vestments over to Eleazar, we learn that God then took the life of Aaron here on the mountain top—this punishment providing a valuable lesson for all those in the priestly hierarchy who fail to preach on a strict abidance to God's holy Word. As Moses and Eleazar descended the mountain that day, we can imagine Moses feeling deeply mortified for having let his frustration get the better of him when he failed to abide by God's instruction to *speak to the rock.*

Continuing with the Israelites' forty years in the wilderness, before leaving the area at the base of Mount Hor the Israelites were attacked by King Arad, a Chanaanite[15] who came up from the land to the south. After Moses appealed to the Lord God for help, the battle was ultimately won by the Israelites who then moved on to the land of Edom. Yet even so, in spite of the good Lord God taking care of His people, as their journeying henceforward became more arduous, the Israelites once again complained out loud—this time even crying out against God.[16] Turning on Moses in their typical way, they accused him:

"Why didst thou bring us out of Egypt, to die in the wilderness? There is no bread, nor have we any waters: our soul now loatheth this very light food."

That we may be given a further lesson, the Lord God sent down among His ungrateful people, fiery serpents that bit and

---

[15] Numbers 21:1-3.

[16] Numbers 21:4-5.

killed many of them[17]—for the snake bites caused them to be burnt with a violent heat. They now cried out to Moses:

"We have sinned, because we have spoken against the Lord and thee: pray that He may take away these serpents from us."

After Moses appealed yet again to his Heavenly Father, we learn[18] that the Almighty told Moses to make a *brazen serpent* and set it up as a sign, such that any who were suffering from the snake bites may be reminded to pray with faith to their Lord God—and live. (Here, the Challoner version of the Douay-Rheims provides an explanation that this was a pre-figurement of the crucified Christ, pointing out the efficacy of a genuine faith in the Divine Son, which will protect one from the hellish bites of the evil serpent.[19])

Thereafter, the Israelites proceeded to a place called Oboth,[20] followed by various other places alternating between wilderness, valleys and desert until they came to the land of the Amorrhites. Here, Moses sent messengers to approach their King Sehon,[21] requesting his permission that they may pass through his land—not to partake of its fruits but simply to pass over to the other side. But the king would not grant them permission and even sent his army to challenge the Israelites, whereupon God in His infinite mercy, once again helped the Israelites to win the battle that ensued.[22] Thereafter God's people dwelt in the land of the Amorrhites until it was time to

---

[17] Numbers 21:6-7.

[18] Numbers 21:8.

[19] John 3:14: *"As Moses lifted up the serpent in the desert, so must the Son of Man be lifted up."*

[20] Numbers 21:10-20.

[21] Numbers 21:21-23.

[22] Numbers 21:24-31.

move on to the land of Basan[23]—where once again they came up against another warring tribe, this time King Og and his powerful army. But the good Lord God told Moses:

"Fear him not, for I have delivered him and all his people, and his country into thy hand: and thou shalt do to him as thou didst to Sehon the king of the Amorrhites."

And sure enough, under Moses' leadership, the Israelites were able to conquer the enemy and take over their land. Hence we see that in spite of God having had to admonish His beloved servant at an earlier date—because of Moses' true repentance over his having disobeyed God's instruction to *speak to the rock*—the Lord God continued to remain with him, looking after him, guiding him, and keeping the Israelites safe.

In due time, God called upon Moses (now 120 years old[24]) to ascend Mount Abarim[25]—and survey the land which He would be giving to His Chosen People. As Moses' eyes roamed across the vast landscape encompassing mountains, valleys, hills and plains, his loving Father went further to gently remind him that he would not live to dwell in this Promised Land. In all humility, Moses then beseeched his Heavenly Father:

"May the Lord the God of the spirits of all flesh provide a man, that may be over this multitude: And may go out and in before them, and may lead them out, or bring them in: lest the people of the Lord be as sheep without a shepherd."

At this the Almighty told Moses to appoint his trustworthy minister Joshua to replace his role as the people's

---

[23] Numbers 21:33-35.

[24] Deut. 31:2.

[25] Numbers 27:12-23.

shepherd—and in their sight, was to lay his hands upon him so that all may know and understand that Joshua would be their new leader. In accordance with God's instructions, Moses went forth and taking his high priest Eleazar with him, called together all the people, and in their presence, dutifully appointed Joshua, his strong and faithful minister, as the Israelites' new shepherd. And Moses told Joshua: [26]

"Take courage, and be valiant: for thou shalt bring this people into the land which the Lord swore He would give to their fathers, and thou shalt divide it by lot. And the Lord who is your leader, He Himself will be with thee: He will not leave thee, nor forsake thee: fear not, neither be dismayed."

Before calling Moses to *sleep with his fathers,*[27] the Lord God, fully aware of the obstinacy of the people and their rebellious ways, instructed His prophet to write down all God's laws in the form of a simple canticle[28]—one that could be sung by the new generation of Israelites to remember all that God had taught Moses, which canticle was to be kept inside the sacred Ark. For indeed, the Almighty shared with His beloved servant that after He would bring His people into the Promised Land of 'milk and honey':

"... they will turn away after strange gods, and will serve them: and will despise me, and make void my covenant. And after many evils and afflictions shall have come upon them, this canticle shall answer them for a testimony, which no oblivion shall take away out of the mouth of their seed."

---

[26] Deut. 31:7-8.

[27] Deut. 31-16.

[28] Deut. 31:19-23.

Forty Years of Punishment
Humility

No doubt deeply saddened by these words, as one final act Moses summoned all the people together[29] and blessed each of the twelve tribes of Israel, reminding them of the infinite goodness of their Almighty God and encouraging them to remain faithful to Him.

Thereafter, we note[30] that God once again led His elderly servant back to Mount Abarim (also known as Mount Nebo), this time to Phasga, a peak to the west which overlooked Jericho—from whence Moses surveyed for the last time the land that God had assigned to His Chosen People. Knowing that his time was come, we can imagine Moses falling to his knees, filled with *humility* (as was his usual way) as he thanked his beloved Heavenly Father for all His many graces and blessings that had helped him throughout his lengthy lifetime.

The Lord God then gently took the soul of His beloved servant—and buried his body in a sepulcher (one that has never been found[31]).

Oh how the new generation of Israelites, survivors of their elderly parents and relations, mourned the death of Moses. For indeed he was already a legend among the people—it being well known that he was a prophet like none other, one whom the Lord God *knew face to face*[32] and with whom He would converse as with a dearly loved friend.

---

[29] Deut. 33:1-29.

[30] Deut. 34:1-5.

[31] Deut. 34:6.

[32] Exodus 33:11; Deut. 34:10.

Chapter 11
THE PROMISED LAND
Hope

With the forty years of punishment over, by way of a final tribute to the great prophet that Moses was, it now seems pertinent to close with a chapter on the Israelites' successful entry into the Promised Land—led by Joshua, the people's new shepherd chosen by God. From the book of Josue[1] we learn that the Lord God spoke to Joshua, saying:

"Moses my servant is dead: arise, and pass over this Jordan, thou and thy people with thee, into the land which I will give to the children of Israel. I will deliver to you every place that the sole of your foot shall tread upon, as I have said to Moses. From the desert and from Libanus unto the great river Euphrates, all the land of the Hethites unto the great sea toward the going down of the sun, shall be your border. No man shall be able to resist you all the days of thy life: as I have been with Moses, so will I be with thee: I will not leave thee, nor forsake thee. Take courage, and be strong: for thou shalt divide by lot to this people the land, for which I swore to their fathers, that I would deliver it to them."

We can imagine the Israelites' new leader filled with encouragement at these words, and lest Joshua not forget the importance of obeying all God's laws, the Almighty continued[2] (His words being a valuable reminder to all those who have been chosen to lead the people in their fight to restore the Kingship of Christ in our fallen world of today):

---

[1] Josue 1:1-6.

[2] Josue 1:7-9.

Josue 6:15-20

The Promised Land
Hope

"Take courage therefore, and be very valiant: that thou mayst observe and do all the law, which Moses my servant hath commanded thee: turn not from it to the right hand or to the left, that thou mayst understand all things which thou dost. Let not the book of this law depart from thy mouth: but thou shalt meditate on it day and night, that thou mayst observe and do all things that are written in it: then shalt thou direct thy way, and understand it. Behold I command thee, take courage, and be strong. Fear not and be not dismayed: because the Lord thy God is with thee in all things whatsoever thou shalt go to."

Now the new generation of Israelites were quick to recognize in Joshua a strong warrior and leader. A man of great faith who, guided by the Hand of Almighty God, they firmly believed would help them to conquer the Promised Land.

In light of their firm confidence, we picture Joshua now standing on a hilltop looking down at the challenging project that the Lord God had placed in his care. The river Jordan ran through the area and beyond that lay Jericho, gateway to the Promised Land. Its walls were thick and sturdy, being built of solid stone, with strong iron gates as the only means of entry. The Lord God then spoke to His faithful servant, outlining His plan for the take-over of the city.

First, God called on Joshua to appoint two strong men to spy out the city.[1] Once night-time fell, after crossing the river (perhaps under the light of the moon), we can imagine the two chosen spies hiding outside the gates until the city had sprung to life, at which time they would be able to mingle with the crowd, hoping not to be noticed amidst the general mayhem of

---

[1] Josue 2:1.

vendors vociferously selling their wares. They would have quickly noticed that Jericho was well guarded, with guards posted at every corner and along the length of the walls—for indeed the Chanaanites had already heard that the Israelites were coming to take over their city.

Come evening the spies had no place to go, but God provided them with help in the form of a good woman, Rahab by name,[2] an innkeeper[3] whom the spies now approached, hoping to take shelter for the night. Although Rahab recognized them as Israelites, she was not afraid of them, for she had previously heard of these people, that they had a powerful God in their lives—and both she and her family were promptly drawn to know more about the Israelites' Almighty God. So she hid them from the guards who had heard that their city had been infiltrated and were going from door to door looking for them.

After providing the spies with dinner (where we can imagine the family's excitement to be making their acquaintance) Rahab led them to a window which overlooked the river (her home, like a number of others, being incorporated into the thick stone walls that encircled the city). With the use of strong heavy ropes, Rahab and her family then helped the spies to escape through this outer window, telling them to hide in the mountains for three days in case the guards should go forth to seek them.[4] But before they left, Rahab begged that their Lord God have mercy on her family and keep them all

---

[2] Josue 2:1-11.

[3] While referred to as a "harlot" in the biblical texts, the Rabbinic texts call her an "innkeeper" based on the *Aramaic Targum*.

[4] Josue 2:15-16.

safe[5]—whereupon the spies gave her a scarlet sash, which she was to hang from one of her windows overlooking the city streets, as a sign to the Israelite army to protect Rahab's home when they came to take over Jericho.

Once back with their leader, the spies told all,[6] whereupon Joshua had the Israelites shift camp from their current location at Setim to an area closer to the river,[7] where they remained for three whole days.

We then learn[8] that the next stage in the divine plan was to have it proclaimed throughout the camp that come the following morning, as soon as the Israelites saw the priests departing from their midst bearing upon their shoulders the sacred Ark (now referred to as the 'Ark of the Covenant'), they were to promptly follow—although not closely but leaving a sufficient distance between themselves and the Ark (two thousand cubits) that the sacred chest may still be in sight. Even as the people would have sensed that something important was about to happen, Joshua confirmed that the Lord God would be working wonders for them[9]—proving that He was in their midst and would be helping them to conquer all the pagan-worshipping nations who were currently occupying the land assigned to them.

True to plan, come the early morn, once the Israelites saw the priests bearing the gold-plated poles of the Ark upon their shoulders, they then followed, keeping their distance as so

---

[5] Josue 2:12-18.

[6] Josue 2:22-23; 3:1.

[7] Josue 3:3-14.

[8] Josue 3:7-10.

[9] Chanaanites, Hethites, Hevites, Pherezites, Gergesites, Jebusites, and Amorrhites.

advised. They watched as the Ark-bearers reached the riverbank, no doubt wondering what they would do. But immediately the two priestly-bearers at the front of the Ark touched the waters with their feet[10] (as instructed by the Almighty so to do)—the riverbank upstream collapsed, creating a dam which at God's Will promptly halted the flow of water. And to the amazement of all who were watching, the priests passed over the resultant dry riverbed. With Joshua leading the way, everyone then followed in their footsteps, crossing over to the other side.

While the riverbed was still dry, as further instructed by the Almighty,[11] Joshua had twelve strong men, one from each of the twelve tribes of Israel, collect twelve large stones from the riverbed, which they carried on their shoulders across to the side where their leader was awaiting them (whereafter God released the dam upstream,[12] causing the waters to rush down and fill the gap). And having set up camp in Galgal on the east side of Jericho, the Israelites were told by Joshua (in accordance with God's instructions) to erect a monument using the twelve stones—by way of commemorating God's miraculous creation of the dry pathway through the river-bed (a miracle not unlike the time when God parted the waters of the Red Sea to allow His people to escape the Egyptians).

God then called upon Joshua to accomplish the next step needed in order to take over Jericho.[13] Summoning the people, Joshua outlined the plan of attack—which indeed was a most

---

[10] Josue 3:15-17.

[11] Josue 4:1-5.

[12] Josue 4:19-25.

[13] Josue 6:9-14.

unusual one. The Israelites listened, wide-eyed, for the Almighty was calling on them to assemble in the form of an orderly procession—first the army up front, followed by seven chosen priests (each armed with a trumpet), with the priestly bearers (carrying the sacred Ark of the Covenant on their shoulders) next in line, and last but not least, the rest of the Israelites bringing up the rear.

Once assembled, at Joshua's command, the orderly procession proceeded to walk towards Jericho, everyone ordered to remain very quiet. (No doubt by this time the guards atop Jericho's walls would have already spotted the Israelites setting up camp on their side of the river Jordan, and fearful of an invasion, would have ordered that the gates be sealed tight, with no person allowed in or out.)

On reaching the city walls, Joshua called for the seven priests to start blowing their trumpets, and the entire assembly, remaining in strict procession and in silence, proceeded to walk all around Jericho (just once), no doubt the sound of the trumpet blasts echoing throughout the city. We can imagine the inhabitants filled with fear, peering out of their windows at the unusual sight, the likes of which they would never have seen before. For six days—the army, trumpet-blowers, and Ark-bearers, followed by all the people—marched in procession right around the city walls with the seven priests continuing to blow their trumpets and everyone maintaining their silence.

Now on the seventh day,[14] the Israelites arose very early and on reaching the city, their procession circled the walls not just once this day, but seven times—while (in accordance with

---

[14] Josue 6:15-20.

the divine plan) everyone united their voices with the trumpet-blowers, and SHOUTED out loud. At this, incredibly, the walls of the city began to crumble—by the help of Almighty God, stone by stone, they steadily hit the ground!

With entry now gained into Jericho, the Israelites were able to take over the city, and in light of its pagan nature, all of the inhabitants and their idols were destroyed at God's command (not Rahab and her family, of course, as they had embraced their new God with joy). Thereafter, with God's help, Joshua continued to conquer the land which God had destined for His Chosen People[15]—always with the presence of Almighty God safely enshrined in the Ark of the Covenant that Joshua had placed inside the sacred Tabernacle which he had set up in the city of Silo in the land of Chanaan.

Now in due time Joshua died, and as God had revealed to Moses, the Israelites forgot their promise to Almighty God and were lured into worshipping the pagan idols of their Chanaanite neighbors—somewhat similar to our world of today as seen in allowing pagan idols to be adored in God's sacred places of worship (as previously mentioned).

We pause for a moment to reflect upon the ill-effects of permitting Satan to rule our lives in this way as we see the godless Socialists continuing to lure our society into following the kingship of sinful man (as prophesied would happen by the Blessed Virgin Mary on a number of occasions when she

---

[15] Josue 18:1.

appeared to various visionaries warning our world to return to Christ[16]).

It yet again begs the question: how much longer will our merciful God be prepared to tolerate such arrogant defiance against the Kingship of Christ before His Arm of divine justice will deliver due punishment on our disobedient world.

Even as we contemplate the seriousness of this question, let us never forget the words of the well-known visionary, Sister Lúcia Santos:[17]

"And let us not say that it is God who is punishing us... on the contrary it is people themselves who are preparing their own punishment. In His kindness God warns us and calls us to the right path, while respecting the freedom He has given us. Hence the people themselves are responsible."

Such a valuable warning for our times! Yet in spite of the possibility of an impending divine chastisement, it is important that God's faithful never lose hope. For even if mankind generally will not heed these words of warning, in due time the good Lord God will provide faithful shepherds—chosen prelates beholden to the traditional Faith of Christ's holy Mother Church—who, with divine help, will unite their voices, along with all God's faithful, and like the shouts of the Israelites accompanying the priestly trumpet-blowers, will

---

[16] When Our Lady appeared as *Our Lady of Good Success* at Quito (Feb. 1594-Dec. 8, 1634), and again as *Our Lady of La Salette* in France (Sept. 19, 1846), and then as *Our Lady of Fatima* in Portugal (May 12, 1982).

[17] Lúcia de Jesus Rosa Santos (Sister Maria Lúcia of Jesus and the Immaculate Heart) (Mar. 22, 1907–Feb. 13, 2005), Roman Catholic Discalced Carmelite nun, visionary of *Our Lady of Fátima*; quotation taken from a letter she wrote to the Holy Father on May 12, 1982.

resound with one accord to bring down all those endeavoring to destroy the traditional Faith.

Thereafter, with the centuries-old traditional Faith once again encouraged and promoted throughout the world, all of the faithful—like Moses when he approached the burning bush on Mount Sinai—will be able to experience God's awesome presence each time they reverently approach Him before the Holy of Holies in the traditional Tridentine Mass of all time.[18]

Then our world will see the fulfillment of the prophecy[19] of the previously mentioned Ezechiel in the Old Testament, repeated in the book of the Apocalypse[20] (New Testament)—which, from the following interpretation, Saint Bonaventure[21] foresaw as a foreshadowing of what would happen to Christ's Holy Mother Church in the last times (which he referred to as the 'future Seventh Age'):

"In the Seventh Age we know that these things happened: the rebuilding of the Temple, the restoration of the city,[22] and peace was granted. Similarly in the future Seventh Age there will be a restoration of divine worship and the rebuilding of the city. Then will the prophecy of Ezechiel be fulfilled, when the city will come down from heaven, not indeed that which is above, but that which is below, namely the Church Militant: when she will conform to the Church Triumphant, inasmuch as it is possible in this life. Then there will be

---

[18] Sermon by Archbishop Carlo Maria Viganò, Jan. 2, 2022, regarding the Holy Apostolic Mass.

[19] The rebuilding of the Temple.

[20] Apoc. 21:2-4.

[21] St. Bonaventure (1221-July 15, 1274), born Giovanni di Fidanza; Italian medieval Franciscan; scholastic theologian and philosopher; Doctor of the Church known as the 'Seraphic Doctor'.

[22] The holy city of Jerusalem; its destruction in 587 BC and its being rebuilt in 515 BC.

the rebuilding and restoration of the city, as from the beginning; and then there will be peace."

We pause again for a moment to ponder on this important prophecy. Saint Bonaventure divided the history of the Church into three periods, based upon the religious orders: first the Monastic orders such as the Benedictines, then the Mendicant orders (Franciscans and Dominicans), and then the *Ordo Futurus* (future order) which would come in the last times.

In this future time of the *Ordo Futurus*, he predicted that the traditional Mass and the social Kingship of Christ would be restored—which he compared to the restoration of the sacrifice in the Temple of Jerusalem once it had been rebuilt in 515 BC after the Israelites' return from their captivity in Babylon (where the sacrifice in the Temple was unable to be offered).

As we are already seeing the persecution of the traditional Faith by the wicked beast influencing our world today[23]—and in light of our good Lord God putting up with only so much before His Arm of divine justice will inflict due punishment on such evil—it would appear that this future Seventh Age of the *Ordo Futurus* is not too far away. Sweet *hope* to shine in the hearts of all God's faithful.

---

[23] As prophesied by Sr. Lúcia Santos in her Three Secrets revealed at Fátima, July 13, 1917.